The Art of Commenting

How to Influence Environmental Decisionmaking With Effective Comments

ELIZABETH D. MULLIN

Environmental Law Institute
Washington, D.C.

November 2000

Copyright © 2000 **Environmental Law Institute**
1616 P Street NW, Washington, DC 20036

Published November 2000.

Printed in the United States of America
ISBN 1-58576-017-X

Library of Congress Cataloging-in-Publication Data

Mullin, Elizabeth D.
    The art of commenting : how to influence environmental decisionmaking
with effective comments / Elizabeth D. Mullin.
        p. cm.
    Includes bibliographical references.
    ISBN 1-58576-017-X

    1. Environmental law—United States—Citizen participation.
    2. Environmental policy—United States—Citizen participation.
    3. Rhetoric.
    KF3775.Z9 M85 2001
    344.73'046—dc21   00-052114

Acknowledgments

The author wishes to thank James McElfish and John Turner of the Environmental Law Institute, James Sandman, and James R. Walpole for reviewing drafts of this book and for their insightful comments and helpful suggestions. She appreciates the awkwardness of commenting on a book on commenting.

Publication of this book would not have been possible without the editing skills of Jael Polnac, the proofreading abilities of Carolyn Fischer, and the production expertise of Linda Johnson and William Straub. The author is grateful for their excellent work.

"Ultimately, of course, it is not better documents but better decisions that count. NEPA's purpose is not to generate paperwork—even excellent paperwork—but to foster excellent action."

—Purpose, Policy, and Mandate, 40 C.F.R. §1500.1(c) (1999)
Council on Environmental Quality Regulations
Implementing the National Environmental Policy Act

TABLE OF CONTENTS

About the Author . . .

Elizabeth D. Mullin has been associated with the Environmental Law Institute as a consultant, editor, and writer since 1994. Before joining ELI, Ms. Mullin was an Assistant Regional Counsel and a Section Chief at the U.S. Environmental Protection Agency in Denver. She has also worked for Arnold & Porter and the Natural Resources Defense Council. Ms. Mullin earned a B.A. from Mount Holyoke College, a master's degree from the Yale School of Forestry and Environmental Studies, and a J.D. from New York University. She is a member of the District of Columbia Bar.

FOREWORD

The Environmental Law Institute (ELI) is delighted to publish *The Art of Commenting: How to Influence Environmental Decisionmaking With Effective Comments*. Seldom does a book fit so squarely within ELI's central goal: enhancing the professionalism and expertise of those who influence or implement environmental laws.

ELI's work reaches a broad spectrum of people. Its information services, publications, and training assist government regulators and enforcers, the judiciary, private lawyers, business executives, corporate environmental mangers and counsel, public interest advocates, academics, and other environmental professionals. At the same time, ELI supports and strengthens citizens and community groups for a constructive, meaningful role in the creation and implementation of environmental laws and policies. ELI provides practical training and clear, useful, and easily accessible environmental information for people who can or want to make a difference.

Elizabeth Mullin's *The Art of Commenting* is a book for everyone who would like to influence an environmental decision. The implementation of environmental laws invariably results in the creation of written documents such as regulations, policies, programs, plans, studies, reports, and permits. A range of companies, agencies, institutions, and individuals may have a stake in how these documents are written and the decisions they support. As described in the first chapter of the book, people within an agency or company writing a document may review and comment on drafts and there may also be a public comment period. *The Art of Commenting* will assist those who are commenting on drafts of their own agency's, company's, or client's documents as well as those participating in the public comment periods available under many federal, state, and local environmental laws.

The book is a practical one. Expertly written by an environmental insider with first-hand experience in the commenting process, the book is a step-by-step guide to writing comments that are most likely to lead to the desired environmental results. Readers will learn how to find background materials to increase their expertise; how best to present and use information; how to write powerful, straightforward comments; and how to follow through once comments are made. From beginning to end, the book is full of useful tips and insight into the politics of commenting.

The Art of Commenting belongs on the desks of both newcomers and seasoned professionals. Students, those beginning careers as environmental practitioners, and members of the public who are new to environmental advocacy will find this book to be a unique and valuable resource with lessons that can ordinarily be learned only through experience. Seasoned practitioners can use the book to hone their skills, think about their commenting strategies in new ways, and help ensure that they are not missing anything. They can also use the book to coach new employees, lawyers, consultants, allies, or others with whom they work. While many readers will use the book to help them prepare comments for submission to government agencies, agency employees who routinely prepare their own comments on environmental documents can use this book to increase their effectiveness.

The active participation of businesses, government agencies, public interest advocates, and concerned citizens leads to better environmental decisionmaking. Each, however, must have the information and skills they need to work effectively. *The Art of Commenting*, written for a wide audience, including lawyers, scientists, engineers, consultants, and lay people, can help increase the effectiveness of anyone working on any environmental matter. I hope that this book will help all of its readers across the country make their voices heard.

—J. William Futrell
Environmental Law Institute

CHAPTER 1:
INTRODUCTION

T his book is about writing, but not just any type of writing. It is about writing to express views on a draft environmental document to improve the document itself or influence a proposed decision.

When a bill becomes an environmental law, it sets into motion a series of actions requiring decisions. The law may require government agencies[1] to adopt regulations, develop programs, prepare plans, conduct studies, write reports, and issue permits. The environmental law itself, or regulations adopted to implement the law, may also apply to the private sector, requiring companies to conduct studies, keep records, or prepare permit applications, plans, or reports for submission to government agencies.

These actions have one thing in common: they all require writing. Someone—in the government, in a company subject to an environmental law, or in a consulting firm working for a government agency or company—must prepare something in writing to comply with the law. It is to this broad body of written work that this book applies. The writings, which may be regulations, guidelines, programs, applications, plans, studies, reports, permits, and the like, are called "documents." The documents may be anything from regulations governing permissible levels of arsenic in drinking water to studies supporting a permit application to build a logging road in a state park. All such documents support or set forth an environmental decision.

---

1. For simplicity, in this book the word "agency" covers all types of federal, state, and local governmental entities, including departments, commissions, administrations, special districts, and others.

Writing an environmental document is tricky business. Environmental decisions invariably involve a complex assessment of scientific, technical, economic, and legal issues. Decisions must often be made despite uncertainties. Time and again, documents must be written even though costs prohibit developing complete data, and there are limits on scientific understanding. It is often difficult to assess risks and predict outcomes, and technology may be unproven. Moreover, due to employee turnover and typical workload allocation patterns, new or inexperienced staffs may wind up with the job of actually drafting the documents.

Both the documents themselves and the decisions the documents represent have repercussions. Technical inadequacies and legal issues in a document can lead to costly delays or can derail an action, particularly if there is litigation. There may be a government enforcement action resulting in fines or even criminal sanctions against an individual or company that falsifies information. The environmental decision itself may have profound effects on human health and the global environment or minor, but important, local effects. Decisions may also have widespread implications for the national or global economy or a serious economic impact on a single company, neighborhood, or resource.

The difficulties of writing an environmental document, coupled with the document's potential environmental and economic consequences, lead inevitably to the activity covered by this book: commenting on drafts of the document. Many different people, organizations, businesses, and agencies may have knowledge that would be helpful or may have a stake in the outcome of an environmental decision. It is prudent to have a variety of people read, evaluate, and provide their views on draft documents before a decision is reached. Environmental professionals recognize the value of this process, which is known as "review and comment."

The review-and-comment process is a cornerstone of the implementation of many environmental laws. Much of the process is internal, taking place well before a document is released outside a government agency, company, or consulting firm. Document writers may well have a team of people, including coworkers, technical advisers, experts, attorneys, and supervisors review drafts of important documents. In large agencies, such as the U.S. Environmental Protection Agency (EPA), the main office or headquarters will invite people in regional offices to review draft documents that may affect their work. Large companies do likewise. To minimize problems with important documents, writers seek to present the best possible information, analysis, and thought before documents are seen by outsiders.

Following this internal review, there may be an opportunity for public comment. The public has a statutory right to comment on certain types of documents, such as proposed federal rules.[2] Many environmental laws require an opportunity for public comment on specific types of documents prepared by the government or regulated entities,[3] and it is agency practice to obtain comments on other types.[4]

This book addresses both the in-house commenting that takes place before a document is released and the formal opportunities for public participation that agencies provide.

---

2. *See* Administrative Procedure Act, 5 U.S.C. §553, *available in* ELR STAT. ADMIN. PROC.

3. *See, e.g.*, 7 U.S.C. §136a(c)(4), ELR STAT. FIFRA §3(c)(4) (provides a 30-day comment period on applications for registration of pesticides that contain a new active ingredient or a changed use pattern).

4. For example, EPA regulations entitled "Public Participation in Programs under the Resource Conservation and Recovery Act, the Safe Drinking Water Act, and the Clean Water Act," 40 C.F.R. pt. 25 (1999), encourage public participation and involvement in rulemaking; issuance and modification of permits; development of information resources, such as citizen guides and handbooks; development of strategy and policy guidance memoranda; and creation of other documents under these three statutes.

The Commenting Process

An environmental impact statement (EIS) prepared in accordance with the requirements of the National Environmental Policy Act (NEPA)[5] illustrates the scope and complexity of the review-and-comment process.

An agency prepares an EIS before undertaking a "major federal action," such as building a highway. The agency begins by holding public "scoping" sessions to solicit comments on what topics should be studied and what alternatives considered. A consulting firm hired by the agency prepares the first draft of the EIS (actually a *draft* draft EIS), usually with sections written by different people. The consulting firm's team leader reviews the entire document and may have comments and questions for the individual authors. A supervisor may review the completed draft before it is sent to the agency that commissioned it. The agency technical staff then reviews the draft and agency legal staff may review it as well. Agency supervisors may comment on the staff comments before they are passed on to the consulting firm. The firm then endeavors to make whatever changes the agency requests, and the entire review process may be repeated until the agency is satisfied.

Once a draft EIS (the true draft, as opposed to the *draft* draft) is completed, NEPA regulations require the agency to request or obtain comments from the following sources:

- any federal agency with jurisdiction or special expertise or authorized to develop and enforce environmental standards;
- state agencies;
- local government entities;

---

5.   42 U.S.C. §4332(2)(c), ELR Stat. NEPA §102(2)(c).

- any Indian tribes that may be affected;
- the project applicant (if any); and
- members of the public.[6]

Agencies must affirmatively solicit comments from persons or organizations who may be interested or affected by the proposed action.[7] Each of these entities may have both technical staff and lawyers review and comment on the draft EIS (and, once again, supervisors who comment on comments). EPA routinely comments on EISs and publishes summaries of its comments in the *Federal Register* each Friday.

Once all these comments are in, the agency or consulting firm prepares a response to the comments and a draft final EIS that incorporates any necessary changes. The draft final EIS is reviewed by the same cast of characters in the consulting firm and the agency and is then revised until the agency is satisfied with the document (which it hopes will be the *final* final EIS).[8] If necessary, there will be a supplemental EIS, and the same process will be repeated.

Federal agencies produce about 500 EISs and 50,000 environmental analyses every year. Sixteen states, the District of Columbia, and Puerto Rico have "mini-NEPAs," and more than 90 countries have environmental impact analysis processes.[9]

In short, lots of commenting takes place—and not only on EISs. This same type of process is repeated over and over, day in

---

6. Council on Environmental Quality NEPA Regulations, 40 C.F.R. §1503.1(a) (1999).

7. *Id.* §1503.1(a)(4).

8. Under *id.* §1503.1(b), an agency "may" request comments on a final EIS.

9. Steve Cook, *Schiffer Sees NEPA Role in Combating Urban Sprawl, Aiding Environmental Justice*, Daily Env't Rep. (BNA), May 1, 2000, at A-1.

and day out, at all federal agencies and in all 50 states, with different types of environmental documents.

Why All the Bother

There is good reason for the central role of commenting in environmental law. Obtaining different perspectives is one of the best ways to improve environmental documents. As discussed above, issues may be scientifically, technically, or legally complex, and the stakes are high—for the public, the companies, and the agencies involved. Obtaining multi-disciplinary internal comments before a document is released outside a company or agency helps to minimize the chance that documents, actions, or projects will be torpedoed late in the process.

Public comments also add a wealth of knowledge and insight to environmental decisionmaking. Members of the general public may know the land, the resources, and the community more intimately than any government agency or consulting firm ever will, and they may have a personal stake in the outcome of environmental decisions. Businesses, which are also members of "the public," have unique and important information and perspectives. The business itself—its owners, shareholders, and employees—may have vital stakes in environmental decisions. Public interest groups, trade associations, and academia can bring valuable expertise that others simply do not have the time or resources to develop.

Consulting with a variety of officials at different levels of government can help government agencies coordinate their work and minimize the risk of duplication, inconsistencies, and costly mistakes.

Overall, environmental protection is a cooperative process that requires concerted action by citizens, industry, and government. For the process to work, each must have specific opportunities to provide information and voice concerns.

Although timely and full participation takes effort and may cause some delay, it is often worth it in the long run. Reviews help to ensure that significant issues are not overlooked. Also, when people are involved early in the process, they are exposed to the many, and often conflicting, factors involved in the decision. Even if they do not agree with a final decision, they may be less inclined to litigate or otherwise fight a decision if they have been part of the process and feel that their views were heard and accommodated. The end result may well be a better decision that can be implemented without further delay.

Even if these lofty arguments do not seem persuasive, the fact of the matter is that public comment is built into all federal and most state environmental programs. It is in everyone's interest to have the best possible comments made.

Why This Book

Anyone can comment, and lots of people do. Unfortunately, many people prepare poor comments. They miss important issues. They bury key points in a dense body of text. They get lost in trivia. They use a format that is hard to follow. They fail to express ideas clearly and convincingly. They do not take advantage of background information that could support their points. They insult the author of the document. Even highly skilled environmental professionals may not communicate their comments effectively. The end result is that the person responsible for document revisions may not make important changes simply because of the way comments were made.

On the other hand, some comments are prepared by seasoned, sophisticated practitioners who have seen many such documents and can quickly and easily review the material, spot issues, and formulate excellent comments.

What about the rest of us? You may be a lawyer, a consultant, an agency staff member, a company employee, a trade association staff person, a nonprofit employee, a volunteer, or a student who is either inexperienced or new to a particular type of document or issue. You may be a private citizen new to environmental activism or new to a particular issue. Maybe you are a supervisor or a mentor responsible for others who do the actual work of commenting. You may work in this field and, to be honest, wish you knew more than you do or simply want to make sure you are doing the best possible job.

This book is for all of you. It is designed to help you learn the tricks of the trade that will enable you to participate as effectively as possible in the environmental decisionmaking process—to find the weaknesses in someone else's document, to anticipate and correct potential problems in your own document, to be heard, whether inside your own organization or externally.

The Art of Commenting

There is an art to commenting effectively, and it is an art that you can learn. The same techniques apply whether the document is a draft regulation, guideline, plan, program, study, report, or permit. The same process applies to federal, state, and local matters, some foreign laws, and even many non-environmental matters. What you say may vary, depending on whether the draft is for in-house or outside review, but the overall approach is the same.

This book will take you through a logical, step-by-step approach to reviewing environmental documents and preparing comments. Chapter 2 discusses how to prepare for a review, including detail on how to obtain background materials that will help develop your perspective and increase your expertise. Chapter 3 provides the nuts and bolts of how to review a document thoroughly and systematically. Chapter 4 discusses the importance of defining your objectives. Chapter 5 gives suggestions on how to organize and write comments. Chapter 6 identifies and discusses major types of comments and includes specific tips and examples of what to say and not to say. Chapter 7 includes steps you can take to follow up on comments you have made.

This book gives you the tools to deal with the worst-case scenario: a thorough document review and preparation of written comments for submission to an outside entity that is likely to ignore or disagree with you. It recognizes that the document itself or the decision flowing from it may be subject to litigation. Fortunately, much commenting does not fit this scenario and throughout the text are specific suggestions for other less intense adaptations.

The techniques outlined in these chapters should increase the quality and usefulness of comments you make. Even if you follow this approach to the letter, you may not get the changes you want. Nevertheless, certain techniques will make it more likely that the person making revisions will understand and be persuaded by your points and make—or argue with supervisors for—the necessary or desired changes.

Even if you get desired changes in the document, you still may not get the substantive outcome you want. If you are after results on the ground, not just a good document, you may have to do more. The remainder of this chapter outlines two steps that can help.

Commenting Early and Often

The best time to influence a document and the substantive outcome that flows from it is before the document is even written. Whether you are an insider or an outsider, your lobbying can begin when you first learn about a contemplated action. Ask for meetings with pertinent staff and decisionmakers about the scope and substance of the document, and put your ideas in writing. Keep in touch to let the pertinent people know of your continuing interest and concern.

The EIS drafting process described above illustrates the importance of early involvement. Much time, energy, effort, and money are spent well before a public comment period begins. By that point, so much has happened that it is hard and expensive to make changes. The President's Council on Environmental Quality recognized this problem and its regulations set forth an elaborate process to try to involve interested people in the EIS process from the very beginning.[10] Yet, key decisions often take place even earlier, with a decision whether to prepare a limited environmental assessment (EA) or a full EIS and in making finding of no significant impact (FONSI) decisions.[11] In this and other matters, it is best to be there from the very beginning saying exactly what you want to see happen and commenting on everything you possibly can, whether it is an agenda, an outline, a concept paper, or an early draft. Raising the big issues early increases the likelihood that they can be addressed.

Finding Legal Help

The purpose of this book is to help level the playing field by equipping everyone—government, consulting firms, businesses, public interest organizations, and citizens—to participate more fully and effectively in the environmental decisionmaking process. Full participation is one way to reduce the likelihood of litigation, which is an expensive and sometimes clumsy way to resolve environmental problems. One need not be or have a lawyer to participate fully in the process. Nonlawyers play a crucial role in drafting and implementing the laws and regulations that form the framework of U.S. environmental law, and they are some of the smartest and most effective practitioners in the field.

But having a lawyer can really help.

In the United States, virtually all environmental decisions and most environmental documents have a legal component.

---

10. The Council on Environmental Quality's NEPA regulations encourage application of NEPA at the earliest possible time, 40 C.F.R. §1501.2(d)(3), and require an "early and open" scoping process to identify the nature and scope of significant issues for an EIS, 40 C.F.R. §1501.7.

11. *See, e.g., id.* §1501.3-.4; Procedures for Implementing the Requirements of the Council on Environmental Quality on the National Environmental Policy Act, 40 C.F.R. §§6.103-.105, .108 (1999).

Even something that looks like a "technical" document, such as a report documenting the installation of a series of groundwater monitoring wells, may also be a "legal" document if it was prepared under the requirements of an EPA administrative order. This very overlap of science, technology, policy, and law makes environmental work interesting and challenging. It also makes it risky from a legal standpoint.

Depending on what you have at stake and your specific role in the commenting process, you may want or need a lawyer. Any good, careful reader can read and understand laws and regulations, but it may be helpful in some cases to have a lawyer identify legal issues, conduct legal research, or help formulate comments. In addition, unfortunately, comments made by a lawyer may carry greater weight than the identical comments made by a nonlawyer. The specter of litigation, which is a great source of stress, a killer of projects, and a sinkhole of time, money, and resources, may draw sufficient attention to a lawyer's comments to make actual litigation unnecessary.

The easiest way to find a lawyer is to have access to your agency, company, or organization lawyers or outside counsel. Otherwise, it takes more work and money.

If you have money, it is helpful to hire a lawyer or law firm with lots of experience working in the area that your document covers. To find such a lawyer, consider the following steps.

- Do a search on the Internet. Check resources such as www.findlaw.com, a legal website with an index of law firms and lawyers you can search by specialty area and location. Also check individual law firm websites, which may have background information on lawyers, descriptions of practices, and information about major clients or matters.

- Look at legal directories, such as Martindale-Hubbell (available in law offices, law school libraries, courthouse libraries, and online at www.martindalehubbell.com), with firm listings and attorney biographies.

- Check local newspapers or journals, such as the Bureau of National Affairs *Environment Reporter* or the *National Law Journal* for articles that identify lawyers or firm names associated with issues similar to yours.

- Contact environmental organizations, industry or trade associations, state or local bar associations, or environmental law professors.

Once you have some names, find out as much background as you can from sources such as those listed above, and then interview several lawyers. An initial meeting is not a commitment to take action, but an opportunity to gather information and explore options. If you like a particular lawyer, ask for names of several clients (or find these on the firm website) and check references. Remember that it is the individual lawyer or lawyers that you will be working with, not the firm, so make sure you are comfortable with the individual.

If you don't have money, or have very little money, there are some other steps you can take. You can try to peddle your matter to one of the national or local industry or environmental groups or to an environmental law clinic at a law school. They too can be found on the Web via sites such as www.findlaw.com. Sometimes such groups or clinics will become involved if the matter is something interesting or important or fits into a niche in which they work or would like to become involved.

You can also seek "pro bono" legal help, free legal help from a lawyer or firm "for the public good." Depending on the arrangement, you may be responsible for out-of-pocket expenses. To find a pro bono lawyer, you can follow the same steps as outlined above for paying clients. Do not hesitate to seek help from the big national firms or the top firms in your area with an environmental practice. They may or may not have a conflict of interest on your matter, and you cannot know without checking around or asking. They may well have a lawyer who would welcome an opportunity to work on your issue.

In looking for legal help, you can ask for a discrete research project or for specific help in reviewing your document. It may be easier to get help for a specific project than for full representation in connection with a matter. This book points out some areas where legal research might be helpful, and you can use these to frame your request.

CHAPTER 2:
PREPARING TO COMMENT

A common approach to commenting is to get a copy of the document, read it, make notes, and write up comments.

This is a big mistake.

Using this method, there is almost never enough time for review. Comments on any given document are always subject to deadlines, and these deadlines, which may be set by internal pressures, a scheduled event, or law, are often tight. For example, there may be as few as 30 days to comment on the supporting analysis and proposed cleanup plan for a Superfund site.[12] Often you will have less time than expected because it will take a while for you actually to get a copy of the document or someone may need to comment on your comments before you send them in. Or you may be busy with other work or have a personal life. In short, without preparation, you may have to scramble to review a thick or complicated document in very little time.

Unless you prepare in advance, you may also lose or fail to maximize your opportunities to coordinate your comments with others. As discussed throughout this book, you can strengthen your position by encouraging federal, state, or local agencies or like-minded individuals, groups, organizations, or businesses to prepare comments or to endorse your comments. Coordination takes effort and time, which you may not have if you are struggling to write your own comments.

---

12. National Oil and Hazardous Substances Pollution Contingency Plan, 40 C.F.R. §300.430(f)(3)(i)(C) (1999).

Before you even have a copy of the document, you can take several steps to set the stage and prepare for your review. This chapter provides a step-by-step guide on how to plan for and organize your work, how to identify and collect background material you might need, how to use the background material, and how to prepare a checklist for your review. It may look daunting. You do not *have* to do it all. But remember: There is a good chance that those on the other side of your issue *are* doing it.

Step One: Set the Stage

At the outset, you will need to identify and coordinate with key people and take steps to ensure that you have enough time for review.

Identify Your Contact

At the very beginning, it is useful to identify a contact for information about the document. This is easy if the author or person responsible is someone in your office or agency. For outside entities, you may have to do some research to find out who the right person is.

For government documents, outsiders should try to get a buddy at the agency. The government is not a monolith. There are one or more agency staffers who know about and are responsible for your document. (Even if government contractors are actually writing the document, a government employee manages the contract and has overall responsibility for the document.) Agency staffers are humans with families, friends, dogs, and interests, and they can help you. To find a staffer to be your agency buddy, call the agency or check the agency website. If the agency has a well-designed and up-to-date website, you should have access to the organizational structure of the agency and a staff directory.[13]

---

13. For a list of federal agency websites, see Appendix A. For NEPA matters, a good starting point is a comprehensive list of agency NEPA contacts in the latest edition of Nicholas C. Yost's *NEPA Deskbook* published by the Environmental Law Institute (ELI). You can access state agency websites either directly or through web linkages, such as ELI's State News and Analysis at www.eli.org or www.findlaw.com.

Be persistent and search until you get the staffer responsible for your document. You may get passed around a lot and even have to call or e-mail several times until you reach the right person.

Plan Ahead

Try to make sure you know in advance, if possible, about contemplated actions that concern you and opportunities for comment. There are two ways to do this. One is to become an "insider" so that you know what's going on. You can be an insider within your own agency or company if you are on the right distribution lists or become part of the grapevine. To obtain insider information on actions taking place outside of your organization, be friendly with other people interested in or responsible for your issue and become part of their grapevine. Stay in touch with your in-house contact or your agency buddy to ask how things are going and when to anticipate any document or action you are interested in. Ask again on the target date, and then the next target date, and so on until a document is ready for review. Early warning about when a document is expected can give you time to clear your schedule for the review, and obtaining the document as early in the review period as possible can give you several additional days to comment.

As word of mouth may not be reliable, those who wish to comment on government documents should also track agency actions. For federal actions, you can track opportunities for comment through the *Federal Register* (see discussion later in this chapter), agency websites, various publications that report on current environmental events, and by placing your name on distribution lists. At the state and local level, it may be more difficult to learn of a proposed action or when to anticipate a document. Although many states lack effective mechanisms to inform the public of opportunities for participation, they all have something. Track whatever mechanism the state does have to convey information about contemplated actions and opportunities for comment, and get on any mail or e-mail lists you can. Some agencies, such as the Louisiana Department of Environmental Quality, have excellent web pages, but in other states, you may have to use several sources, and it may be hard to find exactly what you are looking for or appreciate the significance of material you do find. Even with careful tracking you may learn of an opportunity to comment too late or may miss it altogether, so it is good to stay in touch with your agency buddy as well.

When the document is sent out for review, make sure you know the deadline for receipt of comments. In some cases, timing can be crucial, and late comments will be barred from consideration for legal or practical reasons. Do not hesitate to ask for an extension if you think you will need one. For comments on government documents, regulations may specifically provide for extensions.[14] In other cases, you may need to push for one. You may want to call others you expect to comment (even those who may be on the other side of your issue) and ask for an extension either individually or as a group. In any case, the earlier you ask the better. Don't take extra time, even a day or two, without an extension or your comments may be too late.

Coordinate Your Comments With Others

Depending on the circumstances, you may want or need to plan a strategy to coordinate comments on external documents with others. If you anticipate issues and think it would be helpful, you can ask other federal, state, or local agencies to comment on a document. Comments by EPA, the U.S. Fish and Wildlife

---

14. For example, the Superfund regulations provide that "[u]pon timely request, the lead agency will extend the public comment period [on proposed cleanup plans] by a minimum of 30 additional days. . . ." 40 C.F.R. §300.430(f)(3)(i)(C). Under EPA's NEPA regulations, the "responsible official" may independently extend review periods. Procedures for Implementing the Requirements of the Council on Environmental Quality on the National Environmental Policy Act, 40 C.F.R. §6.401(d) (1999).

Service, a state health or wildlife agency, or other governmental entities are hard for another government agency to ignore. Other agencies can supply information and political pressure, as well as increase the attention paid to your comments.

You may also want to coordinate your comments with like-minded individuals, groups, organizations, or businesses. It strengthens your position, and may increase the likelihood that your concerns will be addressed, if you have others sign, endorse, or adopt your comments. It may also be helpful if others write their own comments, particularly if each of you can raise slightly different issues or if you want to show that many different people or entities support the same position.

In any case, the earlier you plan your strategy, find the appropriate contacts, share information, and coordinate your response with others, the more smoothly things will go. Despite careful preparation, you may find surprises when you actually see the document and will then have to refine your strategy or try a different approach.

Step Two: Identify and Collect Background Material

Even if you enjoy the adrenaline rush of late nights, the quality of your comments will suffer unless you prepare in advance. It is possible simply to read a document and identify anything that seems wrong to you. Many people do this, and you may well spot some important issues. But you may miss even more important ones.

Before you begin your review, it is useful to determine what *should* be in the document. You need to collect and review background materials to develop a clear vision of what the document should contain. What you need will depend on the type of document you are reviewing. Table 2.1 gives some examples of typical environmental documents and the types of background materials you might need to review them. To save precious review time, you can collect background information even before you have a copy of the document, allowing for fine tuning as needed during your review. This preparation will make your review more thorough and your comments more focused.

The starting point for reviewing environmental documents is the law itself—unless you are reviewing draft legislation. It is also helpful to have access to any pertinent regulations; agency materials and guidelines; good examples of the type of document you are reviewing; and substantive materials such as scientific studies, reports, data, analyses, or newspaper clippings. Each of these materials is discussed below.

You do not have to collect *all* of this material. It depends on how much you have at stake, your resources, and the time available. If you work in this field or comment regularly, it is wonderful to have your own copies or ready access to all the pertinent materials. As it is expensive and time consuming to collect material, this guide identifies some ways to gain access to materials that are easy to locate or inexpensive.

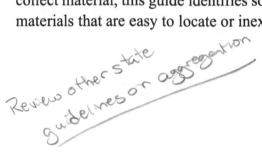

Review other state guidelines or aggregation

Table 2.1 Background Materials for Review of Typical Environmental Documents	
Type of Draft Document	Type of Material
Legislation	Examples of good laws or draft legislation Commentary by academics or others
Regulations	Statute Examples of good regulations Commentary by academics or others
Agency Guidelines	Statute Regulations Examples of good guidelines
Plan	Statute Regulations Guidelines Examples of good plans of the same type
Permit	Regulations Guidelines Examples of other permits
Technical Document	Statute Regulations Guidelines Example of good documents
EIS	Statute Regulations Guidelines Examples of good documents Commentary by academics or others

For comments on any type of document, it is also helpful to have comments prepared by others on the document itself, earlier drafts of the document, or similar documents, as well as background materials, such as studies, reports, and analyses, that help you understand the issues or that support the points you are likely to make.

Handwritten margin note: Is there anything that requires DEP to issue guidance — school for inspectors?

Statutes

Start with the statute.[15] There is at least some basis in law for each type of document. For example, a statute may authorize or require an agency to adopt regulations, develop a plan, prepare a report, issue a permit, or make a determination. Some statutory provisions govern specific types of activities, including activities by private parties (e.g., building a shopping center in a wetland); others require government agencies to do or not do certain things (e.g., developing a Clean Air Act state implementation plan).

> Statutes are legally binding. If the document is not consistent with the statute, there may be grounds for a lawsuit.

At the beginning of your preparation, find and highlight or make note of the pertinent provisions of the statute or statutes on which your document is based. The statute may tell you—often in general terms—exactly what the document must contain. For example, NEPA defines the contents of an EIS, and this language is generally used in the section headings of the document.[16] There may also be a statement of policy or other helpful provisions elsewhere in the statute. Scan the table of contents, if any, for provisions that might contain useful language.[17]

---

15. This book uses the terms "statute," "law," and "act" interchangeably.

16. *See* 42 U.S.C. §4332(2)(C), ELR Stat. NEPA §102(2)(C).

17. The language of §101 of NEPA, 42 U.S.C. §4331, ELR Stat. NEPA §101, and §1002 of the Resource Conservation and Recovery Act, 42 U.S.C. §6901, ELR Stat. RCRA §1001, can bring tears to the eye.

You will need *the exact language* of the statute. Each word is important. For older statutes, such as NEPA, there is an extensive body of case law interpreting the words.[18] For newer statutes, the exact words define how to implement the law, and there may also be new case law.

As discussed under "Pounding the Law" in Chapter 6 ("What to Say"), you can and should quote the statute in your comments. The recipients of your comments are more likely to sit up and take note if you point out a violation of a specific statutory provision. If you can convince the recipients that the law requires a change in the document, they are more likely to make it. And if they don't, you (or someone else) may file an appeal or lawsuit and convince a judge to order the change.

The lawyers among us know how to find the pertinent provisions of law. For nonlawyers or people without ready access to legal resources, the following information may help.

Federal and state environmental laws appear in official code books that can be found in law school, law firm, courthouse, and agency libraries and some public libraries.[19] Various handbooks

---

18. "Case law" is made under environmental statutes when someone files a lawsuit under a particular provision and a judge "interprets" that provision in an "opinion" that sets forth the decision. For example, there is a substantial body of case law interpreting §102 of NEPA, 42 U.S.C. §4332. *E.g.*, NICHOLAS C. YOST, NEPA DESKBOOK, 2ND EDITION 18-24 (1995).

19. The federal government also has a "Depository Library Program" in which the government has placed its publications in more than 1,300 locations across the country. The depositories are open to the public free of charge. Contact your local public library or see www.gpo.gov for the most convenient location.

Law libraries may have the *United States Code* as well as the *United States Code Annotated* or the *United States Code Service*, which contain the full text of statutes and references to legislative history, regulations, and court cases. Although the latter two are not the "official" code, they are a quick way to find helpful background information.

on environmental law contain the full text of key statutes,[20] and you can also find statutory language online through the Internet.[21] To help get you started, Appendix B contains citations to the major federal environmental laws.

Laws are amended from time to time. Make sure you have the latest version.[22]

Regulations

All major federal environmental laws and many state laws are implemented through regulations. Government agencies write and formally adopt regulations, after public review and comment, to expand on and clarify how they will implement a law. Regulations may describe, sometimes with great specificity, what a particular kind of document must contain.

---

20. For example, ELI publishes *ELR–The Environmental Law Reporter*, which includes the full text of numerous statutes. It also publishes deskbooks for each of the major federal environmental laws containing the statute, regulations, and other pertinent materials.

21. The Government Printing Office website (www.gpo.gov) contains the full *U.S. Code*, but this website can be very frustrating. The EPA website (www.epa.gov) is easier to use and contains the full text of major environmental laws under a section called "Laws and Regulations." Other federal agencies have statutes online as well. See Appendix A for a listing of key federal agency websites and other legal resources.

    State laws can be accessed either directly through a state agency website or through links under various other Internet sources, such as State News and Analysis at ELI's website (www.eli.org or www.findlaw.com).

    Please note that the web changes quickly and links appear and disappear on an ongoing basis. Also note that the web does not supply the "official" code, so there may be some errors in the text.

22. The *U.S. Code* website of Cornell Law School's Legal Information Institute has an update service providing recent changes to particular code sections.

> Regulations legally bind both the implementing agency
> and regulated entities. If a document is not consistent
> with the pertinent regulations, there may be grounds for
> a lawsuit.

As discussed above in connection with statutes, recipients of your comments are more likely to open wide their glazed eyes if you point out a violation of, or at least an inconsistency with, a regulation. Again, you will need the exact language.

Always check to see if there are regulations governing the document. The Government Printing Office prints the full text of federal regulations first in the *Federal Register*, published each business day, and later in a bound set of volumes called the *Code of Federal Regulations*, printed each year. Both are available in many of the libraries discussed above and online at www.gpo.gov. Appendix B lists citations for some key environmental regulations, and the EPA website (www.epa.gov) provides access to the regulations that EPA administers. Likewise, state regulations may be found at the libraries discussed above and on the Internet.

Make sure that you have the most up-to-date version of the regulations. Government can move with lightning speed when you least expect it, and you will look and feel like a dodo if you base your brilliant comments on old regulations. Check the *Code of Federal Regulations LSA: List of CFR Sections Affected* and the *Federal Register* or pertinent state indices either manually or on the Internet to make sure that you have the right regulations. You can also call or e-mail your buddy at the agency (see above).

Be aware that the *Federal Register* and state registers may contain proposed regulations. These are clearly labeled as such. Proposed regulations are not binding, but, as discussed in the next section, agencies sometimes use them as guidance.

Agency Materials and Guidance

To assist their own employees, their contractors, the regulated community, and the public, government agencies may prepare (or have their contractors prepare) handbooks, policies, guidelines, memoranda, or other materials to help administer and explain their laws and programs. Sometimes materials, such as proposed regulations or preambles to proposed or final regulations, shed light on particular provisions or issues. At EPA, this material is loosely called "guidance." Other agencies have their own terminology.

In recent years, both federal and state agencies have increasingly sought to use guidance instead of regulations. Sometimes agencies find the open process of rulemaking, with its strict procedural requirements, opportunity for public participation, and potential for legal challenges, too time consuming, burdensome, and controversial. In some states, agency regulations must be approved by a legislative committee or even the entire legislature. Some states tend to promulgate few environmental regulations, unless they must do so to participate in a particular federal program. Instead, agencies may write guidance (which can be written without any public participation at all or with a lesser degree of participation than required for rulemaking) or even propose regulations that are not finalized.

Guidance is not legally binding on the agency or private entities,[23] unless particular guidance is made binding through an administrative order, court order, or consent decree, although at times agencies may seek to treat guidance as a regulation. As a practical matter, agencies give some guidance documents greater weight than others. But don't be surprised if the agency ignores its own guidance. It can and will if it has reason to do so. If guidance supports your position, you can and should use it to bolster your

---

23. *See, e.g.,* Pesticides; Science Policy Issues Related to the Food Quality Protection Act, 64 Fed. Reg. 162, 165-66 (Jan. 4, 1999).

arguments. If it does not, you can seek to persuade the agency to depart from it. Be prepared to demonstrate exactly why the agency should or should not follow its own guidance in your particular instance.

Despite this looseness, it always helps to know if guidance exists for the kind of document you are reviewing, particularly if there are no regulations governing your document. Guidance may provide background material, instructions, examples, policies, and other useful information. Sometimes guidance is very specific and helpful, thus forming a solid basis for your review. In fact, good guidance can let you shortcut virtually all of this chapter as it will give you all the background material you need.

Identifying guidance is sometimes a challenge. EPA alone has hundreds to thousands of guidance documents and does not even fully know what guidance it has. What officially constitutes guidance is a gray area. Some guidance has the word "guidance" in the title, but other guidance may simply be an internal EPA memorandum or even a letter discussing a particular statutory provision or program. The agency wrestles with this beast by trying to compile master tracking systems or dockets of documents that at least someone believes is—or should be—guidance.

If there is particular guidance you want, or if you want to find out what guidance there is, there are numerous websites, hotlines, clearinghouses, dockets, information centers, and libraries that can assist you in identifying and finding the best source for obtaining guidance. Consider the following sources.

☐ *Agency Web Sites.* Agencies have massive amounts of guidance online and information about how to find even more. The full text of thousands of documents can be yours for free.

- EPA (www.epa.gov) offers a variety of ways to obtain access to agency materials, including home pages for each of the Agency's geographic regions and for particular offices within EPA.

- The U.S. Department of the Interior (www.doi.gov) offers a guide and access to information, including a government information locator service index and descriptions of the Department's major information and records locator systems.

- You can also access Government Printing Office (www.gpo.gov) and National Technical Information Service (www.ntis.org) documents, either directly or through linkages with other agencies.

Other federal agency websites and information sources are listed in Appendix A. For state agency information, check the agency website, use ELI's State News and Analysis material and linkages at www.eli.org, or try other Internet sites or search engines to find material.

☐ *Agency Libraries.* Many federal and state agencies have libraries or other resources available for staff and public review. The libraries have dockets and information retrieval systems, and the librarians can help you identify appropriate documents and the best source for obtaining them. Call the agencies or visit their websites to find the location and hours of the library nearest you. If you do not have a computer, agency libraries may have a computer for public use.

☐ *Government Depository Libraries.* Contact your local library, or see for the nearest federal depository library. There are sites across the United States with document collections tailored to local needs.

☐ *Hotlines.* Agencies sponsor (usually through contractors) telephone hotlines where interested people can call with specific questions or information needs. Some hotlines are ongoing, and others are created for specific issues. Use the Internet or call your local, regional, or national agency public information or communications office to find out if there is a hotline pertinent to you.

☐ *Freedom of Information Act Requests.* Under the Freedom of Information Act[24] or FOIA (pronounced "foy-ya"), you can request information from any federal agency, either in writing or in some cases online. To save government resources and search costs for you, agencies request that you first search online for what you want. For more information on FOIA, see Appendix C. Also, most if not all states also have statutes governing the availability of information from state agencies. The request procedures and information provided vary from state to state.

☐ *Nongovernment Sources.* Some nongovernmental sources compile and make available key guidance documents. For example, ELI's Deskbooks on each of the major federal environmental laws include copies of key guidance documents. In addition, ELI's *Environmental Law Reporter* compiles important agency guidance in its Administrative Materials binders. Lists of these guidance documents are classified in a subject matter index and can be ordered from ELI.[25] As discussed above, state materials are also available through the State News and Analysis portion of ELI's website.

☐ *Your Buddy.* You can call or e-mail your buddy, an enthusiastic, industrious, but busy government employee, who can point you to the best guidance or confirm that you have it. Your buddy will probably not, however, give you an exhaustive list of guidance. Depending on the depth of your commitment to commenting, you may want to look independently for more.

---

24. 5 U.S.C. §552, *available in* ELR STAT. ADMIN. PROC.

25. The deskbooks and other periodicals, books, and research reports published by ELI are available through the Institute's website (www.eli.org) or by calling (800) 433-5120 or (202) 939-3844 in the Washington, D.C., area.

One factor to consider in all of this is cost. Online agency documents are free, and sometimes agencies will provide copies of certain materials for free. Other times, if you want a copy of your own or if you use Internet sources that require payment, you will have to pay for materials.

Sample Documents for Use as Examples

Whether you are new to commenting or new to a particular type of document or issue, examples can be of enormous value. These can include examples of a good document of the type you are commenting on or examples of prior comments on the same or a similar document. Examples can both save you time and improve your comments. Sometimes you can lift or adapt blocks of text from prior comments. Examples can also stir your thinking or help you flag or emphasize issues you might otherwise miss, particularly if you read examples before you review your document. They may in fact be the most helpful item in your preparation and may also be the primary advantage that environmental insiders have.

If you work with an agency, a law firm, a consulting firm, or an environmental group, there will often be someone who can help you find examples of good comments. Find someone who has worked in the pertinent area and whose judgment you trust. Do not be afraid to ask. People are flattered to be viewed as experts.

If you are on your own, try to find someone with expertise on your side of the issue through organizations such as a trade association, an environmental group, a citizen's group, or an environmental law clinic. If you don't have an inside track anywhere, try your buddy or call the pertinent agency office or library and ask to see a docket of comments on a particular type of document. You will learn a lot by simply reading through the comments of others.

Substantive Materials and Information

No one comments *just* for the fun of it. All commenters have (1) notice that some type of action will be taken, and (2) something at stake because of the action. The stake may be economic, an effect on business practices, or concerns about health, the environment, or the community.

The substantive materials you need will depend on what you have at stake and what you already know. You may need to educate yourself about the subject matter and potential issues, and you may need to find and present or emphasize material that supports your position. Depending on the circumstances, you may even want to collect and present new information or data.

To gather information, the easiest and perhaps best place to begin is the government itself. We are blessed with an open—and verbose—government, and you are entitled to review the pertinent agency files or records for the matter on which you are commenting.[26] In regulations governing public participation under three environmental laws, EPA itself acknowledges that access to information is "a necessary prerequisite to meaningful, active public involvement."[27] To this end, EPA established a policy for these statutes to provide as much information as possible and for the Agency to make available central collections of documents relating to controversial or significant decisions and provide documents free of charge, where possible.[28] It may be

---

26. The government's own regulations recognize your needs for information. *See, e.g.,* Procedures for Implementing the Requirements of the Council on Environmental Quality on the National Environmental Policy Act, 40 C.F.R. §6.402 (1999) ("EISs, comments received, and any underlying documents should be available to the public . . . .").

27. Public Participation in Programs under the Resource Conservation and Recovery Act, the Safe Drinking Water Act, and the Clean Water Act, 40 C.F.R. §25.4(b)(1) (1999).

28. *Id.*

more difficult to gather information from state and local government agencies. Not all states, nor all agencies, nor even individual agency employees are fully committed to providing complete information to those who seek it.

As part of your search, you will need to find any legally binding documents, such as a consent decree or order, that may govern the contents of the document you are reviewing. You can also learn a lot by reading what others—including industry, environmentalists, internal agency staff, consultants, and other agencies—have had to say. Letters or comments from other state or federal agencies may be of particular interest. As agencies seek to be part of one big, happy governmental family, they try not to pound one another in writing. They can and will, however, point out and discuss important matters. Sister agencies can flag issues, such as the potential presence of an endangered species, which others, including you, can then use as a grenade. Look for these in the agency records.

By becoming an expert using agency documents, you may well know more than the government itself. There may be documents or studies, or an absence of documents or studies, that are worth knowing about. Moreover, just because a piece of paper is in the government files does not mean that the pertinent staffers have read it or appreciate its significance. It is legitimate and highly appropriate to flag issues using agency records.

To find government information, start with the Internet, which may include both general and some site-specific information. The nitty-gritty information about particular matters (such as the toxic waste dump next door) may be found only in agency files. To gain access to these files, you will need to ask. Try asking informally first. (Call your buddy and say "May I please come and review agency files pertaining to _____?") Some files, such as the administrative records for Superfund sites, are readily available to the public through a docket. In other cases, the staffers will just let you come in and go through the files. You may, however, be told to make a formal request under FOIA, as described in Appendix C, or under a similar state statute.

There are also a variety of other sources for substantive materials and information. You can try all the sources listed in the previous section ("Agency Materials and Guidance"), as well as books, journals, newspapers, and other materials in public libraries, law libraries, and technical libraries. You can also try industry groups, environmental groups, and anyone else who might have what you need.

Step Three: Review the Material

If you have any strength remaining, the next step is fairly easy. Simply go through what you have—the materials themselves or the notes you have made—and see what is there. This is your chance to identify and highlight your key materials, learn roughly what you have and where it is, and begin to flag issues. You may want to organize your materials, mark specific text, or make some notes so you can quickly find what you need. At the same time, you can begin work on your checklist as described below.

Note that this can all be done before you even have a copy of the document to review, although you may want to collect some additional material once you have the document in your hands.

Step Four: Make a Checklist

The final step in your preparation is to make a checklist to identify all items that should or must go into the document. Preparing the checklist helps you organize the framework for review so that your review will be systematic and complete. The checklist gives you the big picture of what *should* be in the document, which enables you to do the hardest part of your review—figuring out what is not there, but ought to be.

The form and complexity of a checklist may vary considerably. Depending on how you like to work, the time available, and the type of document, you may simply want a handwritten list of issues. If you review environmental documents for a living or have a lot at stake, you will want more detail. For example, if the contents of a document are defined by complex and detailed regulations, you may want to do a detailed outline with specific cross-references to pertinent material. For more open-ended documents, such as draft legislation or regulations, you will need to do more thinking, and a detailed checklist would be of little use.

In either case, before you spend a lot of time making your own checklist, find out if someone has already done it for you. In the older, more mature environmental programs, there may be excellent guidance that you can use, or someone may be able to give you his or her checklist.

If you are starting from scratch, do the following:

1. Go through the statute to note key language, if any. If the pertinent text is lengthy, you may want to use a scanner or make a copy and cut out the language and tape it on your outline.

2. Unless you are reviewing draft regulations, go through the relevant regulations and note any pertinent language. Again, scan or copy and tape, if you can.

3. If there is any other legally binding document that covers the document you are reviewing (for example, a consent decree or an order), go through that document to identify and note any provisions that would govern the contents of your document.

These three legally binding sets of materials are the most important parts of your checklist. If you don't have much time, stop here and make an outline with these. This will tell you what your document *must* have in it.

If you have more time, expand your outline with helpful text, cross-references, or notes about guidance, examples, substantive materials, and case law. This will help your review be more thorough and systematic, but you can also scramble around later when you are actually going through the document. Indeed, as discussed in Chapter 3 ("Reviewing the Document"), you probably will have to scramble some when you actually see the document and the specific issues it raises.

CHAPTER 3:
REVIEWING THE DOCUMENT

Y ou now have a copy of the document and have, following the exhortation in Chapter 2 ("Preparing to Comment"), completed your preparation. It is time to begin the review.

The first step is to gather your materials: the document itself, your checklist, the materials you collected during the preparation stage, and your office supplies. There are many splendid ways to mark text, from markers to stickies and colored flags. Experiment to find the easiest method for you to highlight text and organize your points for further thought, research, or comment.

Step One: Review the Table of Contents and Skim the Document

Begin by reviewing the table of contents or organizational structure of the document. Then skim the entire document to get a sense of what it does and does not contain. As discussed in Chapter 2 ("Preparing to Comment"), your schedule may be so busy, or your billing rate so high, that you cannot spend much time on reviews. A quick scan allows you to plan and schedule a systematic review of relevant sections so that you can spend your time on the parts of most concern. It may also help you identify early on any additional information, guidance, or expertise you may need. If you will need a reptile expert, it is better to learn that on Day 3 than on Day 27 of a 30–day review period.

Step Two: Read the Document

To review the document, you will have to read it. No way to get around this one.

For a basic review, take the steps listed below. The detail and amount of time spent on the various steps will vary depending on your role in the review process and the time available. You may do a quick review to spot anything egregious or a thorough review to make sure the whole document is sound and well written. You may be interested in a single issue, or you may simply want to check for legal sufficiency. Tailor your review accordingly.

Check the Document Against Your Checklist

Take out the checklist you crafted in the preparation stage described in Chapter 2 ("Preparing to Comment"). Read through the document side by side with your checklist, making sure that each topic on your checklist is covered. If a topic is not covered or not covered adequately (which is common in new areas of law and implementation), this is likely to be one of your major comments. Mark the place in the text and start a list of issues that includes the page numbers indicating where you saw—or should have seen—the issue.

Check for Substantive Errors or Omissions

Look for substantive errors and omissions. In technical documents, you may see errors, such as the following:

- improbable assumptions,
- improper methodologies,
- failure to follow required or accepted laboratory or engineering practices,
- misleading or unclear statements or analysis, or
- unsupported conclusions.

In documents such as draft regulations, guidance, plans, programs, and permits, you may see issues similar to those listed above, as well as legal errors or omissions, inconsistencies, bad policy, poor analysis, and the like.

If you see something wrong, mark the text and add it to your list.

Spot Check for Internal Accuracy

As you read through the document, check for internal accuracy. Do the tables and text match? Is the math correct? Are information and data consistent with the text? Are there inconsistencies between one part of the document and another? Are the cross-references accurate? If you spot check and find inaccuracies, do more checking; the whole document may be sloppy. Add any errors to your list.

Check for Consistency With Other Information You Have

Depending on the scope and purpose of your review, you may want to cross check facts with other information you have, particularly if something seems questionable. For example, you may want to check some quotations, data, or statistics. You may want to check assumptions for a model or run a model yourself. You may want to look up some of the authorities or references cited to see if they are correct and support the stated proposition. If, based on a spot check, you find any errors, check for more. Again, add these to your list.

Step Three: Review Your Notes for Major Problems and Themes

At this point, you should have a document full of colored flags and a pad full of notes that mark and highlight all the issues you have spotted. It is time to go through your list to identify major problems and groups of issues.

After doing so, you may well want to take a second look at your checklist and go through the document once more looking for additional issues that began to percolate during your review. It is easier to solidify your thinking and see things more clearly when you have been through the whole document once. Sometimes you spot new issues, and other times you realize something was addressed later that you had initially identified as a problem.

When this is done, it is time to move on to the next step.

Chapter 4:
Defining Your Objectives

Before you begin writing comments, take time to define your objectives. What exactly do you want to see happen? What are your top priorities? How can your comments help lead to the outcome you desire? Should you comment at all?

Your objectives will vary depending on your role in the commenting process and may include one or more of the following:

- supporting a particular outcome;
- stopping, delaying, or minimizing the impact of an action;
- avoiding an enforcement action or lawsuit by ensuring that the document meets minimum legal requirements;
- preserving a right to appeal a decision;
- ensuring that a document is consistent with your agency or company mission and policies;
- catching technical or substantive errors;
- improving the quality of a document; or
- educating or training an employee, colleague, contractor, or government regulator.

Frame your comments to meet your objectives.

You may decide not to comment at all. Sometimes a document is basically okay or unlikely to change much in the next version so you are comfortable not commenting. Other times, for political, strategic, competitive, or legal reasons, you may prefer to remain silent and let someone else take the lead. Or, you may not want to waste your time unless there is a very serious problem with the document. Even if you think your comments will be ignored, you may want or need to comment anyway. You may be able to effect some change in the document, or you may be required to comment to preserve your option to litigate.

If you decide to comment, set priorities based on your objectives. If you are responsible for an overall quality review, you can and should comment on everything you see fit. Otherwise, focus on what you care about the most. If your comments are too long, you may overwhelm the recipient and bury your truly important concerns amidst lesser ones. As discussed in Chapter 5 ("Writing the Comments"), a good format, with major concerns highlighted and lesser ones set apart, may help alleviate this problem, but overall length matters. Crisp, substantive comments that get right to the point are more likely to be understood and addressed. To get to the point, you have to know exactly what your point is, and so should the reader.

Once you have established your priorities, consider how you will handle other, lesser matters. At times, it is very difficult to judge how picky to be. In some cases, such as in documents that will become legally binding, a single word or phrase can be of paramount importance and being picky is not only appropriate, it is laudable. In other cases, nitpicking can alienate the author and undermine your more important comments. Formatting, as discussed in Chapter 5 ("Writing the Comments"), can help you address minor issues, but you will still need to exercise discretion in deciding whether or not to raise a particular concern.

In general, if you are commenting on an in-house document that will be released to a government agency or to the public, do not hesitate to correct spelling, grammar, or major style errors. You do not want people—whether they are regulators or the public—to think the document is sloppy. If the writing contains errors, people will inevitably think the scientific, technical, and legal underpinnings are sloppy, too. They will want to delve deeper and deeper, all the while thinking: "What else don't they know?" This is not what you want for "your" document. For outside documents, leave the writing errors alone and focus on substance.

CHAPTER 5:
WRITING THE COMMENTS

Sit back and think. Who will be reading your comments? Try to visualize a face, a cubicle or office, a stack of paper, a backlog of e-mail messages, and desktop photos. Is it the person in the office next door, or a giant agency, or a company that you vaguely distrust? How many sets of comments is the person likely to receive? Is it one, five, hundreds, or thousands?

Think a little more. If *you* were the recipient, what comments would you want to receive? The answer to that one is easy. You, like anyone, would like to see the following:

> *Loved* the document! It's *perfect*! Don't change a *single* word!

Anything less is a punch in the stomach and something that the unhappy recipient of your comments (usually the author of the document) will have to deal with in one way or another. Whatever you say is trouble and work.

So, make the job easy.

Hand your comments to the recipient on a silver platter. Present clear, convincing, and easy-to-follow comments appropriate to your type and level of review. State concisely what changes you want and why, if it is not obvious. If possible, give the recipient both what he or she needs to make the revisions and to summarize the comments for supervisors or clients. Persuade as necessary.

The remainder of this chapter gives tips on how to prepare formal, written comments on a major environmental document.

There are suggestions on how to present yourself t46hrough a cover letter or memorandum, how to organize and format your comments, what to do and what not to do regarding style, and how to frame your comments to increase the likelihood that your concerns will be understood and addressed. For short or informal comments, you will probably not need to go this far. Tailor these suggestions to your specific needs and your role in the commenting process, and use what is helpful.

Once you have thought about how to frame your comments, move to Chapter 6 ("What to Say"), which addresses the substance of your comments (i.e., what to say, rather than how to say it).

Cover Letter

Formal comments should begin with a cover letter for external documents and with a memorandum for in-house documents. The cover letter or memorandum should address the elements described below.

Tip One: Clearly Identify the Document Reviewed

The document you are commenting on may be one of many the agency or company is preparing, or it may be one of many drafts of the same document. Your cover letter or memorandum should clearly state the author, the exact title, the date, the control number or docket number (if any), and any other identifying information for the document you are commenting on. Otherwise, you may have wasted your time preparing comments.

Tip Two: Establish Your Authority to Comment

To ensure that your comments are given appropriate weight by the recipient, your cover letter or memorandum should establish who you are. In many instances (particularly for internal documents), this can be done simply by inclusion of your name and job title or position and organization. The recipient may understand and accord due respect to your comments based on this alone.

Sometimes, however, more information is helpful and appropriate. If you represent a company, briefly describe what the company does and why it is interested in the proposed action. If you are with an organization such as a citizen's group or trade organization, in a sentence or two describe your organization, how big it is (e.g., number of members), what it does, and its experience in the issues covered by the document. For organizations that are not well known to the recipient or potential readers of the file, provide more detail. If you have special expertise or unique knowledge that should increase the weight accorded your comments, include that. Sometimes people include a brief description of their expertise or even a curriculum vitae to establish their authority to comment. People who are simply concerned citizens should describe as specifically as possible why they have knowledge, expertise, or a concern about the proposed action.

If you are strengthening your position by endorsing, joining, or coordinating with the comments of others, indicate this in your cover letter or memorandum.

Tip Three: Include Any Pertinent Commenting History

If your comments are part of a series of comments you have made on earlier versions of the same document, the same type of document, or the same issue, you may want to say this and, if appropriate, provide a cross-reference to or a copy of earlier comments. Do this only if necessary to establish your authority to comment, or if you want to piggyback on your prior comments.

Tip Four: Identify Attachments, If Any

Your cover letter or memorandum should clearly identify any attachments you have enclosed. It is easy for documents to become separated and misfiled. The cover letter can alert the reader to search for any missing pieces.

Tip Five: For Lengthy Comments, Briefly Summarize Your Major Concerns

If your comments are long or complex, it may be helpful to summarize and highlight your major concerns. Use bullet points for this, with no more than one sentence in each bullet. These are important for a reader simply scanning for big issues and positions taken.

Organization and Format

The organization and format can make or break your comments. Using a good format makes your comments easier to understand and use, lets the recipient discern what you are after, and can even increase your credibility. Most importantly, however, it helps ensure that your key points don't get lost in your verbiage.

The organization and format of your comments should clarify your points and make the important ones stand out. Use subject headings to focus the reader, and, if you have anything more than a few minor comments or one major comment, organize your comments into two parts. As described below, the first part should identify and highlight your major concerns. The second part should follow with page-by-page, section-by-section, or issue-by-issue comments identifying the specific points in the text you want changed. Overall, your comments should look like they come from an experienced, knowledgeable professional or member of the public.

Tip One: Use Headings

The use of subject headings is a quick, easy way to make your comments stand out. Even if yours are the only comments on a draft internal document, headings make your comments more comprehensible and help draw attention to key points. This is even more important when your comments are one among many. A government agency may receive hundreds to thousands of comments during a public comment period. For example, the National Park Service received 1,355 letters and 5 petitions commenting on a proposed rule pertaining to the Kaloko-Honokohau National Historic Park in Hawaii.[29] If you are circulating a copy of your comments to encourage others to join or endorse your comments, headings will make it easier for them to figure out whether they agree or disagree with your list of and position on issues.

Even within a set of comments, commenters often address more than one issue. Let's say EPA receives 50 sets of comments on a draft Superfund Remedial Investigation/Feasibility Study. One letter may comment on groundwater contamination, traffic associated with implementation of the selected remedy, and health issues. A second letter may comment on cost, air quality, and traffic. A third may comment on groundwater and remedy effectiveness. A fourth may comment on all these issues, plus four others. And so it goes.

When agencies receive multiple sets of comments on a range of issues, they must organize the comments in order to make sense of them. The most effective comments reflect the process agencies use to organize the comments they receive. Federal agencies (or their contractors) go through the comments, either electronically or on paper, to identify categories of comments and concerns. They make changes in the document as appropriate and may prepare a summary of and response to each major comment.[30] The summary discusses revisions made or reasons

---

29. Kaloko-Honokohau National Historic Park, Hawaii; Final Rule, 64 Fed. Reg. 19480 (Apr. 21, 1999).

30. For examples of agency summaries and responses, see preambles in the *Federal Register* for final EPA regulations.

why a comment was rejected. The summary may say "Many commenters noted" or "Six commenters recommended" to give a sense of how many shared a concern or how many approved or disapproved of a particular topic. These summaries are organized issue-by-issue in the order of the original document, with headings and subheadings.

Your comments need to make the recipient's job easy. Don't make recipients or their contractors wade through paragraphs or pages of your prose to identify and separate out each issue you want addressed. Do it for them. Perhaps your brevity and clarity will so impress them that they will use your comments as the basis for their summary of the issue.

The examples in Table 5.1 of the first sentence of a comment illustrates how headings can be used to identify the topic or even to hammer home your point.

Table 5.1 Effective Use of Headings	
Less Effective	**More Effective**
The risk assessment grossly underestimates the chemical's possible effects on human health.	**Risk Assessment.** The risk assessment grossly underestimates the chemical's possible effects on human health. or **Risk Assessment Understates Risk.** The risk assessment grossly underestimates the chemical's possible effects on human health.

Topic headings are appropriate and helpful for comments of any length on any document, external or internal. If your comments will be one of many sets of comments, it is probably best to use headings to editorialize so that your point will be clear. However, this approach may be a bit heavy-handed for in-house comments on an early draft where a simple identification of the topic will do.

For lengthy comments, it may be helpful to use both headings and subheadings to organize your points. Consider numbering your subheadings to help ensure that the recipient does not miss a point in lengthy comments.

Tip Two: Prepare General Comments

If you have anything more than a few minor issues or one major concern, formal comments should open with a section entitled "**GENERAL COMMENTS**," "**MAJOR CONCERNS**," or something of the sort. This section should identify and highlight the document's major deficiencies, concisely describing the nature of the problem, why it is important, and what should be done about it. As discussed above, each general topic should contain a heading.

"General Comments" are good for both you and the recipient. The discipline of writing this section forces you to organize your thoughts and focus on what is important. Having to identify and articulate the big-ticket items helps you realize what they are. This section also eases the recipient's burden of figuring out what is important, what big changes may be needed, and how to summarize issues for supervisors or clients.

This section also helps ensure that you do not bury your most important concerns somewhere in the middle of your comments where they may never see the light of day. The example in Table 5.2 demonstrates this technique.

Table 5.2	
Effective Use of General Comments Section	
Less Effective	**More Effective**
13. On page 12, there appears to be a word missing in the second sentence of the first full paragraph. 14. Adoption of the proposed regulation would immediately shut down all coal-fired power plants in the United States. 15. The map reproduced on page 56 is blurry.	**MAJOR CONCERNS** **Catastrophic Disruption of Power Supply.** Adoption of the proposed regulation would immediately shut down all coal-fired power plants in the United States.

For informal comments (such as those from a supervisor or in-house peer reviewer), for fairly minor comments, or for a set of comments with each comment of approximately equal importance, a list is fine. Any special concerns can be highlighted in a cover note.

Tip Three: Write Page-by-Page Comments

The document reviser (usually the author) will sit with the document and go page by page to make changes. Make it easy. You know what you want, so don't make the reviser guess or hunt around for the right place.

If you are commenting on any lengthy document (i.e., more than two to three pages) or have more than one concern, follow your General Comments with more specific page-by-page or section-by-section comments. This gives you a place to add less important or more specific points to your major concerns. Alternatively, you may want to go issue-by-issue in the order in which issues arise in the document, using headings and page numbers if needed. Your approach will depend on what looks best and is clearest; you may want to adjust the format when you have finished the first draft of your comments and see how they look.

Page-by-page comments help direct the reviser to the places in the text where changes are needed to deal with your major concerns.

> Always identify the specific places to address your major concerns. Include a cross-reference to the pertinent part of your general comments, and, if it would be helpful and not repetitive, a one or two sentence summary of your major concern.

Cross-referencing your major concerns is essential. Otherwise, an energetic and careful reviser may go point by point through your specific concerns and carefully address each one, totally ignoring that wordy, introductory stuff at the beginning (i.e., your major concerns).

Table 5.3 shows an example of how to handle cross-references in page-by-page comments.

Table 5.3	
Effective Use of Cross-References	
Less Effective	**More Effective**
§9. See "General Comments" above.	§9. See the comment on "Public Participation" on pages 4-5 of our General Comments.
§9. Thirty days would be better.	§9. Given the likely length and complexity of the draft resource management plans, the bill should allow at least 30 days for public comment. Currently the bill provides for only 14 days. See pages 4-5 of our General Comments.

Do not repeat your entire General Comment, unless it is very short. Your goal is to help out the reviser as much as possible without making your comments unnecessarily long.

For formal comments, you may wish to include headings on some or all of your page-by-page comments. As discussed above, headings can be very helpful.

Tip Four: Make Your Comments Easy to Read

Commenting is an art. If you don't have a good graphic eye for what looks professional, find someone who does. Let him or her advise you on a good format and how to set up your document so that it is easy to read and looks nice. You can also read through some comments by others, see what you like, and copy that format. Once you have prepared one set of comments, you can use the same format over and over again. In picking your format, consider the tips listed in Figure 5.4.

Figure 5.4

Formatting Tips

- Do not hand write your cover letter or memorandum or your comments. This undercuts your credibility.
- Use a good, clear, easy-to-read typeface or font (not too small).
- Make sure your margins are big enough (one inch on each side and on the top and bottom).
- Use enough space to avoid dense blocks of text.
- Avoid simply numbering your comments (e.g., 1, 2, 3, 4 . . .), which may either make them all look equal when they are not or give a false sense of priority to more-or-less equally important comments. Consider using unnumbered headings instead. As discussed above, it may help to number subheadings so the reader does not get lost between headings and subheadings in lengthy comments.
- Have your detailed comments track the structure of the document you are commenting on. Use chapter or section headings, including section numbers, if that would help the recipient of your comments quickly understand your point.
- Highlight headings and subheadings using both spacing and a combination of capital letters, bold font, underlining, or italics to make sure that both your organization and your points leap off the page at the reader.
- Provide a table of contents, preferably with page numbers, for long comments.
- Minimize your use of footnotes. Most people don't read them.

Once you have a good format, think about its continuing integrity. Many people now want to send and receive electronic comments, and this can be quite a good thing. A printout of such comments may, however, change the spacing, margins, or pagination, rendering your format less clear and less easy to read. For formal comments, particularly if they will become a matter of public record in an agency docket, you may want to submit comments in both electronic and paper format. That way both the recipient and the docket users will have the benefit of your best work.

Style

This section cuts right to the quick of style techniques that may enhance the effectiveness of your comments. If you had Miss Edwards in the Fifth Grade, you can skim this section. You know all about writing. If you want to go beyond what is here, there are entire books on writing style, all worth reading.[31]

Tip One: Use Topic Sentences

Each new comment and each paragraph should begin with a topic sentence.[32] A paragraph is a distinct unit of thought, usually a group of sentences that contribute to a central idea. Each sentence should relate to the other sentences in the paragraph and the sentences should all fit together into a logical progression. The topic sentence expresses the central thought of the paragraph and is therefore the most important sentence.

The two paragraphs in Table 5.5 demonstrate the effective use of topic sentences. The topic sentences are underlined. The other sentences add to or clarify the thought, but are not the central idea.

---

31. For general writing tips, see WILLIAM STRUNK JR. & E.B. WHITE, THE ELEMENTS OF STYLE (1959). Lawyers and people who aspire to write like a good lawyer should read one or more of the legal writing manuals, such as NORMAN BRAND & JOHN O. WHITE, LEGAL WRITING: THE STRATEGY OF PERSUASION (3d ed. 1994); LYNN B. SQUIRES ET AL., LEGAL WRITING IN A NUTSHELL (West Publishing Co. 2d ed. 1996); RICHARD C. WYDICK, PLAIN ENGLISH FOR LAWYERS (3d ed. 1994).

32. Each separate comment is like a paragraph in that it is a unit of thought. Several paragraphs may make up a comment on a particular topic or issue.

Table 5.5

Examples of the Effective Use of Topic Sentences

The capacity of the proposed wastewater treatment plant is insufficient. The design plan assumes a population growth of 1,000 people a year over the next five years. The county's projections, which are the best numbers available, indicate likely growth of 10,000 people per year. If this is the case, the population would exceed the capacity of the proposed plant before construction is even completed.

The costs of the reclamation plan far exceed any conceivable benefit. The draft plan would require expenditure of $10 million to revegetate 6 acres of land. Located in a heavily industrialized area, the land has virtually no potential for wildlife, recreation, or any other nonindustrial use. The area needs vegetative cover to control erosion, not landscaping.

As in the examples in Table 5.5, the topic sentence should come first. The recipient may well skim your comments. When people skim, they are most likely to read the first sentence of a paragraph and, if you are lucky, the last sentence. Unless you have really caught their eye, they skip the rest.

When you have completed your comments, go through your draft and read just the first sentence in each comment and/or paragraph. These sentences should *all* be topic sentences. The first sentences should be a summary of the main points of your comments as a whole. They should flow together in a logical progression so that if the reader reads *only* those sentences, he or she will know exactly what your comments are about. It is best if most of your topic sentences state exactly what is wrong with the document or what changes are needed. Avoid the temptation to begin a paragraph stating or describing what the document *does* contain. The bored recipient will probably be thinking "I know that" and skip the remainder of the paragraph.

If any of your first sentences are not topic sentences, reorganize or rewrite them. In some cases, you will need only to move the topic sentence. In other cases, such as in the examples in Table 5.6, where topic sentences are underlined, you will need to do a little editing when you move the sentence.

Table 5.6 Effective Use of Topic Sentences	
Less Effective	**More Effective**
The draft EIS contains a lengthy discussion of the possible impacts on wildlife. Nowhere, however, does the document address the Preble's meadow jumping mouse.	The draft EIS fails to address possible impacts on the Preble's meadow jumping mouse.
This tiny mouse hibernates for nine months. In the summer, it emerges only at night, when it moves through tall grass leaping four feet in a single bound and may thus elude carefully placed traps. It is very difficult for biologists to determine whether or not this species is present in the study area.	It is very difficult for biologists to determine whether or not the mouse is present in the study area. This species hibernates for nine months. In the summer, the tiny mice emerge only at night, when they move through tall grass leaping four feet in a single bound and may thus elude carefully placed traps.
The proposed permit conditions would require construction of a new outfall. More time is needed. It will take us at least 30 days to hire a contractor, prepare a design, and obtain the materials. The construction itself may take at least two weeks. We need at least 60 days to complete the work properly, but the proposed conditions would give us only 21 days.	The proposed permit conditions provide inadequate time for construction of a new outfall. It will take us at least 30 days to hire a contractor, prepare a design, and obtain the materials. The construction itself may take at least two weeks. The proposed conditions would give us 21 days, but we need at least 60 days to complete the work properly.

Tip Two: Use Short Sentences (50 words or fewer)

Your writing style can either help or hurt your comments. Good, crisp writing makes your points effectively; wordy, convoluted writing bores, distracts, and confuses the reader.

People go overboard with words. Often they are in a hurry, and it actually takes more time and thought to be concise. Some people think they sound smarter or have more persuasive arguments if they use nice, big sentences with lots of phrases strung together with commas. Other people love their own language and can't bear to cut even one carefully crafted clause.

Take the time and effort to be brief. Count words yourself, or use the grammar function of your word processor to highlight sentences longer than 50 words. Or, try reading your comments aloud. If you run out of breath during a sentence, it is probably too long. Break any long sentences into pieces, and eliminate the excess, as in the example in Table 5.7.

Table 5.7
Effective Use of Sentences

Less Effective	More Effective
Given the noise level of the all-terrain vehicles, the visual impact of seeing all-terrain vehicles in the natural splendor of the park, the adverse effects on wildlife in the area, and the impacts on the trail system, in its proposed plan all-terrain vehicles should be kept out of the park by the Park Service.	The proposed plan should exclude all-terrain vehicles as they are noisy, harm wildlife, damage the trails, and undermine the natural splendor of the park.

But don't go too far. Some commenters may be too brief. Be sure you use *enough* words to convey your points. If you are making an important point, more than a sentence or two will be needed to (1) make the point, (2) indicate its importance, and (3) explain it adequately for the reader who may not have your knowledge and expertise. Do not be like the engineer hired for a complex and expensive water quality assessment who wanted simply to present his clients with a table that he thought would speak for itself. It *might* speak for itself to another engineer, but it most assuredly did not speak to his nontechnical clients who wanted to understand the problem in their creek.

Tip Three: Use the Active Voice

Virtually every sentence of your comments should be written in the active, rather than the passive, voice. The verb (action word) in a sentence defines its voice. A verb with a direct object is in the active voice; the subject *does* something.

    Commenters slam the document.
    Subject   Verb Object

    The author sweats bullets on the revision.
    Subject   Verb   Object

Conversion of the direct object in the above sentences into a subject creates the passive voice; something *is done.*

    The document is slammed by commenters.
    Subject   Verb

    Bullets are sweated by the author on the revision.
    Subject Verb

The subject of each of the above sentences is passive (something is done to it), and neither has a direct object. Such sentences are longer, more complicated, and weaker. The passive voice is like that. Wimpy.

Table 5.8 shows some examples, with the verbs underlined.

Table 5.8 Use of Active Voice	
Passive Voice	**Active Voice**
More than 20 acres of wetlands <u>would be destroyed</u> by the proposed project.	The proposed project <u>would destroy</u> more than 20 acres of wetlands.
The economic effects on neighboring businesses <u>were not taken</u> into account by the planners.	The planners <u>did not take</u> into account the economic effects on neighboring businesses.

When you have finished your draft, go through it to look for the passive voice. Your word processing grammar check function may highlight the sentences for you. If not, try a search key or actually search with your eyes for compound verbs, which are always necessary for the passive voice. Rearrange or rewrite as many of the sentences as you can so that you make your points rather than having points made by you.

While you are looking at verbs, make sure yours are powerful ("is" is the weakest verb there is). Your comments should be full of verbs such as those listed in Table 5.9.

Table 5.9 Strong Verbs	
Fails	Strengthens
Underestimates	Lacks
Overestimates	Undercuts
Disregards	Undermines
Understates	Excludes
Overstates	Neglects
Ignores	Exaggerates
Weakens	Oversimplifies

Ask the reviser to move, rewrite, clarify, change, eliminate, add, delete, or expand.

Tip Four: Do Not Ask Questions

One of the biggest style mistakes commenters make is asking questions. Commenting is not a conversation. Rather, you are telling the recipient of your comments what to do. Some commenters are lazy, and other commenters, who may not be comfortable barking orders, ask questions to be nice. If you want to be nice, say please, and then tell them what to do.

When you ask a question, you give the recipient an out. As mentioned above, recipients want to make no changes whatsoever. They either ignore questions completely or answer them in their head. Sometimes you can see their lips silently forming the answer. In any case, you get nothing on paper.

When you have a question, it really means that either (1) the text is unclear, or (2) you have a problem with something that is or is not stated. The examples in Table 5.10 illustrate how to handle situations when you have an irresistible urge to ask a question.

Table 5.10	
Effectively Making Points Without Asking Questions	
Less Effective	**More Effective**
Does the second sentence in paragraph two refer to the hairy or the downy woodpecker?	Please clarify whether the second sentence in paragraph two refers to the hairy or the downy woodpecker.
Are air emissions an issue?	The text should indicate whether air emissions are an issue and, if they are, discuss them.
What about the impact on wetlands?	The EIS should address the impact of the proposed project on wetlands. or Agency regulations require the EIS to address the impact of the proposed project on wetlands.

Tip Five: Be Respectful

Your comments should always be respectful. Even if the document is ill-conceived, unintelligible gibberish, a real human being with feelings worked to prepare it, and a real human being with feelings (probably the same one) now has to deal with your comments. It is not in your interest to alienate this person, particularly if he or she is your employee, contractor, client, teammate, attorney, coworker, or agency buddy.

Always take the high road on paper and in e-mail. In addition to showing civility, always assume (even if you do not really believe this) that the author's heart is in the right place and that he or she simply needs more information or political clout to do the proper thing. You can then supply the information and, if possible, some clout.

Never call anyone's integrity or motives into question. Moreover, it is a mistake to suggest that government employees are not doing their job or living up to their agency's mission. For example, many, if not most, professionals at EPA work there because they want to protect the environment. They are understandably prickly about criticisms that suggest that they are not doing this. Likewise, many in the private sector want to do the right thing. Be firm, dignified, and respectful in your comments on any document.

When you have an overwhelming urge to rant, try to pretty up what you are really thinking. Table 5.11 contains some examples.

Table 5.11 Conveying A Respectful Message	
Less Effective	**More Effective**
You are completely out of touch with reality.	The conclusions do not reflect a full understanding of the economics of the mining industry.
You call yourselves the Environmental Protection Agency!	The proposed standards do not go far enough to protect sensitive aquatic organisms.
Quit whining.	The first paragraph in the company's "Waste Disposal History" description should be deleted. People are likely to view it as self-serving.
You think only of the bottom line and don't give two hoots about future generations.	The document should contain a more complete and realistic assessment of possible long-term impacts.

Chapter 6:
What to Say

There are many different types of environmental documents, and the issues they present may vary widely. How can a general book such as this one possibly address the content of a specific set of comments? It can't. No book can tell you what to say about a particular document. Your comments will depend on the following:

- your role in the commenting process (e.g., supervisor, peer reviewer, lawyer, concerned citizen),
- whether it is "your" document or an outside document,
- the type of document,
- the overall quality of the document,
- the substantive issues,
- the stage of revision (first draft or nearly ready to go out),
- the likelihood that your comments will be addressed,
- the sensitivities of the recipient of your comments,
- who else is reviewing it and for what,
- how many sets of comments are likely,
- whether the matter is or is likely to be in litigation,[33]

---

33. Exercise caution with comments on in-house documents concerning matters that may be subject to litigation. Your comments may be released outside your office inadvertently, through discovery, or, in the case of government agencies, through FOIA. *See* Appendix C. Remember that draft and final documents, as well writing on your computer and e-mail messages, are all potentially discoverable or subject to FOIA.

   You may be able to protect your comments from release if a discovery privilege or FOIA exemption applies. If you are working on a matter where litigation is ongoing or possible, make sure you know whether an exemption from disclosure applies and, if so, how to make sure your comments stay within that exemption.

- how much time you have,
- the resources available to you,
- what you know or can find out, and
- what you care about.

And probably a lot of other things. That is why commenting is an art.

The following tips will give you some ideas on how to frame your comments. As you write, use these tips and the Table of Contents of this book as a checklist to help ensure that you are not missing anything important.

Tip One: Make the Strongest Possible Points

One of the first things law students learn is the following adage:

> If the law is on your side, pound the law.
> If the facts are on your side, pound the facts.
> If neither the law nor the facts are on your
> side, pound the table.

One or more of these strategies may be effective, depending on the circumstances of your document. Each is discussed below.

Pounding the Law

Although all three strategies may work, the law is probably your strongest argument, if you have it. As discussed in Chapters 1 ("Introduction") and 2 ("Preparing to Comment"), nearly all the environmental documents on which you are likely to comment have a basis in law. The "law" may be one or more provisions from a statute, a regulation, a binding or useful court decision, a court order, a consent decree, an administrative order, or another source of legal authority. Any of these authorities may establish requirements that govern the substance of the document and the actions that flow from it.

A document may thus have two types of legal problems. One problem may be with the document itself (e.g., it left something out, it did not address something adequately, it included something it should not have, it went too far or not far enough, or some other problem). In short, it did not meet the letter or intent of a legal requirement governing the content of the document. Alternatively, the problem may be with the proposed action described by the document (i.e., the action itself or some aspect of it would violate a legal requirement). Either problem can be a violation of law, and both are fair targets for your comments.

Any potential or actual violation of law is a *HUGE* comment. As discussed at length in Chapter 2 ("Preparing to Comment"), violation of a legally binding requirement may be grounds for a lawsuit that can delay or derail the proposed action. That may be a good or bad thing depending on your role in the commenting process. In either case, it should be placed under the "Major Concerns" section of your comments for all to see.

To make your comment, you must specifically describe or quote the pertinent language, include a citation, and discuss the violation. Table 6.1 provides some examples of how to do it.

Table 6.1	
Effectively Pointing Out Violations of the Law	
Less Effective	**More Effective**
The proposed sampling sites are not representative.	The proposed sampling plan is inconsistent with 40 C.F.R. §141.21. Under this provision, public water systems must collect coliform samples at sites that are representative of water throughout the distribution system. The proposed plan excludes those portions of the distribution system where coliform contamination is most likely due to the age and condition of the equipment. The sampling sites are therefore not representative of the system.
The old farm at the end of our street has a rich and interesting history and possibly many artifacts.	Under 40 C.F.R. §6.301, EPA must take steps to preserve historic resources. The old farm at the end of our street has a rich and interesting history and possibly many artifacts. At a minimum, there should be a historical survey to assess the property and mitigating measures to preserve anything of historical or cultural value.
The completion report is not sufficiently descriptive.	The completion report fails to meet the requirements of Section XVIII of the Consent Decree requiring submission of a "detailed" report that fully documents the work undertaken. The single paragraph submitted is not sufficiently descriptive.

Your expertise and your role in the commenting process will influence how you raise legal concerns. Some commenters, including lawyers, members of the public, and agency employees with either legal or technical backgrounds, can and should raise legal concerns clearly and directly on most types of documents.

Nonlawyers working for consulting firms or companies should be more careful about how they raise or articulate legal concerns. The clients, or company lawyers, may not want to hear an engineer's legal opinion or conclusion, particularly on a draft internal document. On the other hand, much important work is handled by environmental professionals who are not lawyers and yet are really the experts in the implementation of environmental laws. If nonlawyers see a legal issue, they can and should flag it carefully as in the example in Table 6.2.

Table 6.2 Effectively Raising Legal Issues	
Less Appropriate	**More Appropriate**
The completion report violates Section XVIII of the Consent Decree.	Section XVIII of the Consent Decree requires submission of a "detailed" report that fully documents the work undertaken. The agency is not likely to view the single paragraph as sufficiently descriptive.

Nonlawyers who are not sure whether to raise a particular legal issue, or how to articulate it, should first check with the firm or company lawyer to see how to handle the matter.

There may be some divergence of viewpoints about when to raise legal issues. In general, the sooner the better, particularly on in-house documents. Good decisionmaking depends on having the best possible information, and it is a better process when problems are identified as early as practicable. It may be tempting to hold back and spring a surprise issue late in the game, hoping to delay or derail an action you don't like. This may well backfire, however, and delay raises the stakes, increases antipathy, and lessens the likelihood of cooperation for a good solution.

Pounding the Facts

A second strategy for commenting involves the "facts," the substantive information underlying the action or decision. There are three primary types of problems with facts.

- Information is presented, but it is wrong or misleading.

- The information is incomplete, either because pertinent information was not included or because new information is needed.

- The facts are presented, but not relied on or given sufficient weight in the decision.

Most arguments with environmental agencies over implementation issues are won, not on the law, but on technical arguments.[34] Factual problems may be relatively minor ones that simply make the document look sloppy. On the other hand, they may be important issues with major consequences for public health or the environment or the people or businesses concerned.

Many environmental documents and decisions rely on an intertwined complex set of facts and law. Law and regulations govern both the information that must be collected and the information that can be considered by the agency in its decisionmaking. For example, when an agency needs to make a decision concerning cleanup of contaminated soil, it must consider a

---

34. *See* DAVID SIVE & FRANK FRIEDMAN, A PRACTICAL GUIDE TO ENVIRONMENTAL LAW 7 (1987).

whole series of facts: the nature and extent of the contamination, the threat posed by the contamination, the appropriate level of cleanup, the technology to be used, where and how to dispose of the contaminated soil, and many other issues. There may be both legal questions and technical problems, issues, and uncertainties associated with each element of the decision. It is highly appropriate for commenters to raise concerns about any of these issues.

In framing comments and determining the appropriate degree of emphasis, it is important to distinguish legally relevant facts from other facts. Some facts are legally relevant while others, although perhaps of great concern, are not legally relevant. For example, the potential of a project to destroy a wetland is a relevant fact because there are legal safeguards (or some would say hurdles) in place to protect these resources. A project's potential to destroy a beautiful vista (e.g., the view of the ocean from your beach house) is probably not a legally relevant fact, as private views are generally not a protected resource.

If your major issues and concerns hinge on legally relevant facts, your comments are straightforward. As discussed in Chapter 2 ("Preparing to Comment"), based on your review of the pertinent law, regulations, and other legal authority, you will know or can learn the information the document must contain for the action or decision. Make sure the document includes the pertinent information and that the decision or action reflects appropriate reliance on this information. If it does not, make your comments accordingly. The most valuable comments provide important factual information not known to or not fully understood by the author of the document. As discussed later in this chapter, you must be careful and credible when providing new information or telling an author he or she is wrong. In addition, comments on documents that rely on risk-based decisionmaking routinely and appropriately question assumptions, methodologies, and conclusions.

Sometimes you may want to influence a proposed decision or action because it threatens a resource you care about, your property values, or your business. There may be no law that directly protects this interest. In such cases, people may look for a surrogate issue where there are legally relevant facts to delay or derail a project or action. It may well be that a citizen's group cares more about the rural character of a beautiful farm region than it does about a rare plant that lies dormant underground for 17 years before it blooms, but the group may use whatever factual, legal handle it can to influence a decision. Likewise, a chemical company may go to great lengths to question and attack the science behind a regulatory standard, not for the love of scientific integrity, but because it wants to avoid the costs of compliance with the proposed standard. These indirect approaches are less comfortable for those involved, and they may lead to public cynicism. Cases such as these are ripe for a broader consensus-building approach, open to all with an interest in the issue.

Pounding the Table

A third option is pounding the table. There are a variety of ways to do this, but the two most popular are attacking the process and attacking the people.

Attacking the process is always fair game. As discussed in the "Why All the Bother" section of Chapter 1 ("Introduction"), process *is* important, and failure to follow a good process can create problems for both in-house and outside documents. At times, the statute or regulations define the decisionmaking process and provide specific points for public participation. For example, the Superfund regulations contain detailed provisions governing the timing and nature of public involvement in cleanup decisions.[35] Failure to follow one or more of these provisions is a

---

35. National Oil and Hazardous Substances Pollution Contingency Plan, 40 C.F.R. §§300.430(f)(3), .435(c) (1999).

violation of law. Even when law or regulations establish participation requirements, there are times when agencies can, should, and in fact will do more than the law requires. Likewise, for private sector documents, a good process can save time and money in the long run.

Most process-attacking comments will fall into one of the following categories:

- There was inadequate notice of the opportunity for involvement.

- There was not enough time for review.

- The right people were not involved (e.g., particular experts or affected people or entities were not consulted or included).

- The format of involvement was inadequate (e.g., there should have been a scoping meeting, a workshop, roundtable discussions, a facilitator, an advisory group, a working group, an open forum, a meeting in a different place or at a different time, additional time for comment after a meeting, or some other process).

- Not enough background materials were available for meaningful participation.

- The docket excluded important documents.

If appropriate, your comments should recommend a more open or inclusive process. In recent years, some agencies have experimented with or adopted a working-group approach to environmental decisionmaking, bringing people together to work out a solution for particular problems or regulatory issues. This may at times be a good approach, but may also exclude people who have an important stake in the matter. As discussed in Chapter 2 ("Preparing to Comment"), people may not even be aware of the proposed action, or they may be deliberately excluded to facilitate resolution of the matter. When important interests are not involved in a decision, problems invariably arise.

An attack on the competence or integrity of the people involved is a trickier option. Commenters frequently question the work of the technicians, experts, scientists, and laboratories involved in environmental work. Collecting data, planning, conducting studies and analyses, and engineering can be quite difficult, and it is easy to make mistakes or have differing interpretations. It is appropriate to evaluate and question this work and, in general, problems can be handled through comments on the facts. At times, it may also be appropriate to question whether the right person or firm or expert or laboratory is conducting the work. They may in fact be doing a bad job, or there may be someone who is better. This is an easier, less risky comment to make when you are questioning the competence, experience, and expertise of a hired outside expert, consulting firm, or laboratory. It is a harder comment when the person is your own employee or teammate or a government employee with whom you have an ongoing regulatory relationship. In these instances, much delicacy is needed.

On rare occasions, people may pound the table with personal attacks, such as alleging a lack of integrity, a conflict of interest, or bad faith. This is a desperate measure, which may make it difficult or impossible to develop or maintain a good working relationship with the targeted person or organization. It is, of course, appropriate to raise a legitimate concern, if there is a real and important problem. If instead it is merely an attempt to play hard ball, a personal attack will probably hurt your reputation, your agency or company or clients, and your interests in the long run. It may make you look bad even to your friends or allies if you make allegations when you are unsure of the truth and importance of what you say.

Tip Two: Suggest Specific Language When Possible and Appropriate

In general, it can be very helpful to suggest specific language changes. If you know exactly what you want, you can and, in many cases, should say so. This saves time for the recipient, who will not have to think of the right words to address your concern. It also helps ensure that your concerns are addressed the way you want them to be. Otherwise, a revision may add new problems or simply make things more complicated than they need to be.

For in-house documents, mark ups are a quick and effective way to provide specific language changes or even comments. Placing word changes on the document itself or on copies of specific pages saves time for both the commenter and the recipient. The commenter does not have to type the old and the new language, and the recipient can go straight to the place where changes are needed without having to wade through the document to find, for example, the second sentence in the first partial paragraph on page 28. Just make sure that your markings are clear, and attach additional sheets if you have a lengthy insert. If you have a lot of changes or complex changes, it is helpful to retype that portion and provide an electronic copy. Your goal is to be clear, not to run the recipient through a maze.

Mark ups are not always a good idea. They should never be used for public comments on government documents and are inappropriate for any other formal comments. They should not be used even internally for long documents, unless you mark the specific pages with flags so comments will not be overlooked. They also should never be used if you think there may be many sets of comments on the document. They are best used for comments on in-house documents under 100 pages.

If you cannot or should not use a mark up, you can type specific language changes in the page-by-page section of your comments clearly indicating where the changes should go. If you have the capacity on your word processor, you can use the "redline" and "strikeout" functions as in the examples in Table 6.3 to illustrate the exact changes you want.

Table 6.3 Suggesting Specific Language	
Less Effective	**More Effective**
Delete the words "high levels of" and add "at rates higher than indicated on the label" after the word pesticide.	Rewrite the sentence to state: "Application of the pesticide at rates higher than indicated on the label could harm the monarch butterfly." or Rewrite the sentence as follows: "Application of ~~high levels of~~ the pesticide <u>at rates higher than indicated on the label</u> could harm the monarch butterfly."

It may not be appropriate to suggest specific language in some instances. At times, the reviser needs the discipline of having to figure out how to address your comment and making the changes in his or her own words. This is the case when you want to make sure people *really understand* what change is needed and *agree with it.*[36] This does not always matter, but sometimes it does. For example, a lawyer commenting on a technical document may see the need to say certain things to meet a legal requirement. The scientist or engineer revising the document may be thinking, "I don't really agree with this, but the lawyer says I have to say it." Then, during the deposition or on the witness stand, the author

---

36. For example, ELI sometimes comments on proposed environmental laws and regulations in foreign countries. In such instances, it is better to explain the issues and alternative approaches than to recommend specific language that may not be fully understood, either because of language differences or because of differing legal experience and traditions.

say, "I don't agree with this, but the lawyers made me put it in." This is not a good situation.

To avoid this problem, in some instances you need to explain the issues carefully and suggest an approach, instead of providing specific language changes. If people really understand each other's issues, it may be fairly easy to draft language that will satisfy everyone. For important issues, it is good to check the next draft to make sure your concerns were understood and addressed.

Tip Three: Indicate What You Support as Well as What You Disagree With

At times, it is helpful to comment on what you support as well as what you disagree with. When you are commenting on an internal document and generally agree with most of it, just say, "The document looks great. I have attached some general comments and some specific suggestions. Please call me if you have any questions." An outsider commenting on a controversial issue, particularly during a public comment period, needs to do more.

It is possible that an agency will change things you like as well as things you don't like in the final document. The premise of this book is that comments can in fact produce changes in documents and in decisions. That is what comment periods are for. That is why you are commenting, and that is why others, even people who disagree with you, are commenting too. It is therefore helpful to identify and support the things you like. If you are silent, the agency may assume you don't particularly care one way or another.

You need not spend a lot of time and effort supporting what you like. A sentence or two as needed is sufficient, unless you have good information or arguments you think no one else will raise, or unless an action is controversial and you think the author may cave under pressure from other commenters. Also, this is one of the few occasions where your topic sentence can say something nice—a welcome relief from relentless criticism.

If someone requests comment on specific issues within a document and you have an opinion, by all means comment.[37] When someone truly wants viewpoints, they may be very receptive to yours.

Tip Four: Give Specific Examples to Illustrate Concerns

A mental picture is worth a thousand words. When possible, use examples to clarify and illustrate your points. The example may be a hypothetical, a real-world example, or a comparable example. Such examples are more vivid and more persuasive than a mere statement. If you have facts or studies to add, use them. If not, provide simple examples or hypothetical situations to illustrate your concern. Table 6.4 provides some examples.

---

37. *See, e.g.,* Pesticides; Science Policy Issues Related to the Food Quality Protection Act, 64 Fed. Reg. 162, 165 (Jan. 4, 1999).

Table 6.4
Using Examples and Hypothetical Situations

Less Effective	More Effective
Construction of the proposed parking lot would increase the amount and speed of surface runoff into the stream, exacerbating the existing flooding problem.	Construction of the proposed parking lot would exacerbate the existing flooding problem. In February, it rained two inches over a 24-hour period. As the enclosed photograph indicates, the resulting flood nearly reached the high school track. The new lot would increase the amount and speed of surface runoff into the stream, leading to more frequent and larger floods and increase the likelihood of flood damage.
The company underestimates the economic benefits of waste minimization.	The company underestimates the economic benefits of waste minimization. As the attached article indicates, XYZ Corporation adopted a similar program two years ago and has already recouped the cost of the program and realized additional savings of 10 percent.

Tip Five: Provide Supplemental Information, If Needed

As suggested in tip four, it may strengthen your comments to provide supplemental information. You may well have compelling facts, studies, articles, or other information that the document's authors did not have or did not use. It is in your interest to point out or provide whatever information you think they should have used but did not.

Make sure that you supply solid, well-documented information, including everything the recipients need to assess its quality and reliability. It is *not* helpful to provide the following:

- information without supporting details;

- pages copied from a book, article, or other publication without a complete citation to the source (author, title, date, publication, volume number, page number, and any other identifying information);

- photographs without at least an approximate identification of the date, photographer, and location;

- results of a study without a copy of the study or a description of or references to the researchers, the assumptions, the study itself, and the dates.

The recipient can and should ignore your information unless you supply complete and sufficient documentation to permit an evaluation of its accuracy.

Exactly how much information to provide is a tricky question. As discussed above, your goal is to make revisions as easy as possible. It is easiest by far if you provide full paper copies of everything, highlighted and marked with tabs to draw attention to the key parts. The reviser can simply go to the information and start making the changes you want. It is exhausting to search files, go to the library, make phone calls, or even use the Internet, which often does not work as well or as quickly as one would hope. The more work it is to dig out the information, the less likely it is that it will be found and used.

Yet, there is a cost to supplying complete information. It may be expensive to buy or make copies, and you will, of course, need to respect U.S. copyright law.[38] Moreover, particularly if there are lots

---

38. Basic information on U.S. copyright law can be found on the U.S. Copyright Office web page at www.lcweb.loc.gov/copyright/.

of commenters, the recipient does not want and will not read two feet of material from you. You will need to exercise some judgment.

A few pointers for dealing with supplemental material are listed below. First, think about what information the recipient is likely to have readily accessible.

- If it is something that is widely available to environmental professionals, such as a statute, regulations, important agency guidance, major periodicals, and other such sources, don't provide a copy. You can always quote or refer to the pertinent language and provide a citation. If you don't think the recipient can reach a copy within 50 feet of his or her desk, include an Internet citation if you can.

- If the information is not widely available, or if you think it is *really, really* important, provide a copy or a description of where the information can be readily obtained.

- If you are not sure whether the information is accessible to the recipient, you can always call or e-mail and ask. For agency documents, see Chapter 2 ("Preparing to Comment") for tips on how to find a government agency buddy.

- Lastly, you can offer to provide a copy if the recipient contacts you. But don't hold your breath. He or she will probably just blow it off.

Table 6.5 provides some tips on how to supply information.

Table 6.5
Effectively Supplying Supplemental Information

Less Effective	More Effective
Many people in my neighborhood have died or are suffering from this rare form of cancer.	Many people in my neighborhood have died or are suffering from this rare form of cancer. These include [give as many names and addresses as possible]. In addition, I have heard about [give whatever other information you have.]
The agency has allowed this approach in other instances.	The agency has allowed this approach in other instances. In 1999, it approved a similar element in four plans. Appendix 3 (Tab 3) contains a list and short description of these plans.
The operation of aging commercial nuclear power plants poses an ever-increasing threat of accidental release of radiation.	The operation of aging commercial nuclear power plants poses an ever-increasing threat of accidental releases of radiation. [Summarize construction and accident history, with citations to fuller descriptions.]

Tip Six: Offer Helpful Solutions

The best comments offer solutions to the problems raised. It is not always possible to do this, but to the extent you can, point out a solution to the issues you identify. To develop a solution to complex issues about which there are differing concerns, you will need to understand your own concerns, the concerns of the document's author (such as time, budgetary constraints, and institutional concerns), and the concerns of other interested parties. You know your own priorities and concerns and may know those of others. If you don't know or are not sure what the concerns of others are, ask them.

Once you understand the differing concerns and priorities, try to craft a solution that addresses them. Sometimes there is no middle ground or solution that will satisfy everyone, but often there are one or more solutions. Options may include changes in the timing of an action, mitigating measures, offsets, conditions, emergency exemptions, or other such solutions. Conflicting sides may not get everything they want, but that is true no matter what approach is taken.

Your comments need not necessarily offer a total solution, but suggestions that give the recipient something to work with may be of enormous value.

CHAPTER 7:
WHAT NEXT?

You have finished and sent in your comments on time. You have cleaned off your desk. You have taken a little breather. Now what?

The ball is in their court. Now is the time for the recipients to deal with your comments. Perhaps they will thoughtfully and appropriately address each and every one. Perhaps they will address some and not others. Perhaps they will ignore them completely. It is up to them.

Or is it?

If you *really* want your comments addressed, you may want to or need to do more. Exactly what you do depends on the type of document you are commenting on, your role in the commenting process, and whether you have commented on an internal or external document. This chapter discusses some options.

Comments on Internal Documents

There are several ways to follow up on your comments on your own company's or agency's documents. The easiest way is to ask to meet with the recipient to discuss specific issues, answer any questions about your comments, and ask how any big changes might be handled. You can also ask to see the next version before it goes out to make sure the revised document in fact addresses your concerns. This may well take care of everything.

For important changes, it may be necessary to do some internal lobbying. Some changes may cost a lot of money, affect important deadlines, or relate to legal risk. For example, a comment recommending additional studies may lead to both expense and delay. If you encounter resistance to changes you believe are essential, you may need to provide additional substantiation for your views and find allies for your position. If necessary, you may also need to go up your organization's chain of command on either or both the legal side and the technical or business side.

Public Comment on Agency Documents

For outsiders commenting on agency documents, there are a variety of ways to influence an agency decision before, during, and after a public comment period. As discussed in Chapter 1 ("Introduction"), the best time to influence a document is before it is even written. Even if you become involved later in the process, there are a variety of ways to voice and reinforce your views.

Option One: Review Other People's Comments

Following the tips in Chapter 2 ("Preparing to Comment"), you can ask to look at the comments others have submitted. It is always helpful to see what other people say. You may have missed some important points. You can weigh the relative strengths and weaknesses of various comments. You can also identify the people or groups who disagree with you, as well as potential allies. This may enable you to develop a more effective follow-up strategy.

Even before the end of a public comment period, you can ask to see anything that has already been submitted. Many people wait until the last minute, but you just might luck out and see something helpful.

Option Two: Submit Additional Comments

If you missed anything or would like to defuse comments of the opposition, you can submit additional comments. Although you may be outside the comment period, submit them anyway. The agency may ignore you. It may not, if you make really good points. There is nothing to prevent you from sending a letter, and it may get you somewhere. Note that the agency may reopen the public comment period and give all sides a chance to say more. Just make sure your foot stays in the door.

Option Three: Speak at Any Public Meeting or Hearing

Ask to speak at any public meeting or hearing. Invite your friends, allies, and experts to attend and, if appropriate, speak. If a meeting or hearing is not scheduled, and you think there should be one, by all means request one. If there are limits on your participation (e.g., some states have jurisdictional requirements), find someone who can participate who shares and can voice your concerns.

Your oral comments should be a summary of your major concerns, emphasizing and explaining the most important points. Don't just read your written comments on the document. It is, however, a good idea to write down what you are going to say and submit the text of your oral statement to the agency. This way, it gets the benefit of your comments twice and an accurate and accessible rendering of your statement. Also, you get the benefit of writing them twice, which invariably, no matter hard you try the first time, makes them better. When you have to write as if explaining something to a live human, you nearly always make improvements, thinking of something to add or a better way of phrasing what you did say.

After the meeting, you often think of something you wished you said to either improve your own comments or respond to points made by someone else. Do not hesitate to send a follow-up letter and request its inclusion in the record. It can't hurt, and it might help.

Option Four: Rally Support for Your Position

If you have not already done so and think it would help, rally support from federal, state, or local agencies or officials or from businesses, organizations, or citizens groups that could bolster your position. Support from others may make it harder for the agency revising the document to ignore you.

Option Five: Lobby Your Buddy

After your comments are in, it is useful to call your staff-level buddy for a chat or a meeting. (If you don't already have a buddy at the agency or don't have the right buddy, see Chapter 2 ("Preparing to Comment").) This is your opportunity to discuss your concerns, offer information, ask questions, discuss other people's comments, or push for another draft or a supplement. You can try to learn how the agency is likely to address comments and find out what the next step is, what the timing might be, and who the decisionmaker is. If your buddy is willing to talk, you may learn information that will help you plan your next steps.

Try to win your buddy over to your point of view. Most agency matters are handled at the staff level, often by inexperienced staffers. It is helpful to have your buddy on your side, particularly if you will have an ongoing relationship on this or other matters. You want your buddy to be fully informed about your point of view, understand, and, if possible, share your concerns. You also need to be a straight shooter whom your buddy trusts and respects. You can push hard for your views or even file a lawsuit, but it does not help you or anyone in the long run if you mislead or seek to threaten or intimidate your buddy during the administrative process.

Be aware that your buddy may take notes about your conversation that may become an official agency document. Government employees may prepare a memorandum based on these conversations (usually entitled a "Record of

Communication") for inclusion in agency files or the administrative record for the decision.

Option Six: Meet With the Decisionmaker

After meeting with your staff-level buddy, you may want to do more. Your buddy is probably not the official decisionmaker.

In the federal government, there is an official decision maker for each formal agency action. Agencies are creatures of law and can act only when Congress, or in some cases the President, has given them authority to do so. The statute creating an environmental law typically authorizes or requires "the President" or "the Secretary" or "the Administrator" to take an action. The person holding this office then formally delegates the authority down the chain of command. The delegations move one step at a time within the agency (including regional offices), until a person holding a specific position receives the delegation. Occasionally, there are conditions on the delegation, such as consultation with someone up the chain. When a statute says "the Administrator shall," it may in fact be a Division Director in each EPA region that ends up with the delegation to make the decision or take the action. States also have official decisionmakers, but there are generally fewer supervisory layers, so there may be either no delegations or less complex ones.

Sometimes agencies have a solid, unified viewpoint on a particular issue. In general, unless there is a significant error in policy or judgment, supervisors will back their staff, which is why it is crucial to seek staff support. Other times, the staff and the decisionmaker may have differing views, and this divergence may even be present in the supervisory layers in between the two. Ultimately, it is the decisionmaker who has to agree with you, and you will need to bring this person over to your side.

If you don't already know, find out who the decisionmaker is. You can ask your buddy, who should know exactly who the decisionmaker is and whether there are any conditions on the delegation. You can ask if any other outsiders have met or are planning to meet with the decisionmaker. Alternatively, you can also ask to see a delegations manual (if there is one), which contains the documents setting forth the formal delegations and redelegations of authority for each official agency action. You can then find out the name of and contact information for the decisionmaker.

If you want to go over your buddy's head to consult the decisionmaker, it is advisable to let your buddy know first, except in the most extreme cases.[39] Such a meeting may antagonize decisionmakers, who are used to this type of maneuvering. And it *will* antagonize the staff, which may make it more difficult for you to achieve your short-term goals and may harm any ongoing regulatory relationship with agency. To minimize the problem, call your buddy and say, "We really hate to do this, but this decision is extraordinarily important to us. We feel we really have to talk directly with so and so, and we are arranging [or have arranged] a meeting." This may smooth ruffled feathers. They will be even smoother if you ask to include your buddy in the meeting.

Who comes to the meeting is a delicate matter. If you plan to bring a lawyer, let the agency know so it can have a lawyer also. If you are going up the agency chain of command, you should also go up your chain to achieve some degree of parallelism in the relative power of people at the meeting. It may be inappropriate for staff-level employees of outside entities to meet with agency decisionmakers and vice versa. Sometimes the decisionmakers will want to get together alone for a power talk. Staff on both sides hate this, and good decisionmakers won't do it. It is better to invite all pertinent staff, supervisors, and decisionmakers. This makes for a big meeting, particularly if both sides bring consultants, but it is worth it. Everyone has full information and invests more in the process, which is important in the long run.

---

39. *See* SIVE & FRIEDMAN, *supra* note 34, at 4.

Sometimes decisionmakers will say no to a meeting. This may be because they are busy, they don't care about you or your issue, or they rely heavily on and want to empower their staff. They will probably refuse to meet if the particular decision must be based on a written administrative record and they cannot hear information outside the record. In this case, all your written work and administrative lobbying needs to have taken place earlier in the process.

Option Seven: Involve a Legislator

If a decisionmaker does not appear to care about you or your issue, or if you think your views on an important matter will not prevail, you may want to contact one or more members of Congress, a state legislator, or local officials. Depending on the issue, you may want to contact either your own representatives or those with expertise in the area, sympathy with your point of view, or both.

At a minimum, you can ask your legislator to write a letter to the agency asking the agency to explain its action or urging it to take a particular action. Be sure to supply the legislator with accurate information on the issue as well as with information on what you want to have happen (a substantive result, a meeting, reopening the comment period, a more open process, or other outcome), not just your own one-sided viewpoint. Often legislative staff will write a letter for the legislator's signature. The agency (probably your buddy) will probably prepare a response relatively quickly. (Federal agencies have special personnel handling Congressional inquiries, and they track the letters like they do FOIA responses.) If you have made any misstatements or have provided incomplete information, the agency will point this out in its response and undermine you.

Involving elected officials will increase the heat, if not the light, on your issue. It puts the agency into a tizzy, giving you both staff and management attention. You may even go up the chain past the decisionmaker this way. Political pressure is more likely to help you at the state or local level, where the legislature is responsible for the agency budget and close ongoing contact is necessary. It is less successful with federal agencies, which are more insulated from outside politics.

If your issue is important and you fear an unfavorable outcome, it would be helpful to consult someone with experience or expertise in lobbying or legislative affairs to plan your strategy.

Option Eight: Go to the Press

Another method to bring attention to your issue and increase pressure on the decisionmaker or his or her boss is use of the press. This can be done in a lot of ways, depending on your issue and the profile you want.

You will need a press strategy for any but the simplest issues. In planning your strategy, you should do the following:

- identify the target audiences (national, state, local, the agency itself, or your own members or employees);

- determine the best media or combination of media resources to reach those particular target audiences (Internet, television, radio, newspapers, magazines, an employee or member newsletter, flyers); and

- determine the timing and content of the message you want delivered.

The content may be the hardest part. If you are going to write your own article or op-ed piece, you have control over the content. If you are feeding information to a writer who will cover or write the story, you lose control. The writer may misunderstand or misrepresent what you say, or may do independent research that results in a story that goes against your position. The writer controls the angle and the story itself.

You can and should present information to the writer that helps build the story along the lines you want to see. You can write an outline, talking points, or a description in your own words and provide useful background materials. You can also provide other contacts that might be helpful.

Whether you are talking to National Public Radio or your neighborhood newspaper reporter, your material must be accurate and your solutions viable. It will not help your position to have an irate, but misinformed, public demanding impossible or inappropriate action. Under these circumstances, the agency can, should, and may well ride out the storm and do what it thinks is right and possible. And your credibility will be shot.

Conclusion

This book presents some of the time-honored tricks of the trade used by environmental professionals who play by the rules. Use of these approaches will enhance your effectiveness and increase the likelihood that you will be heard. Even if you don't achieve all of what you want on a particular document, you may well make some progress on the issue that will make a difference in the long run. You may also help to establish or confirm yourself as a skilled, competent, clear-thinking, effective environmental professional: in short, a force to be reckoned with. This will serve you well down the road.

APPENDIX A:
AGENCY WEBSITES

This appendix includes a list of websites for federal agencies that routinely produce environmental documents or may have information of interest. Note that the Internet changes constantly and, by the time you read this, these and other citations provided may have changed, and new and better information may be available.

Department of Agriculture	www.usda.gov
Department of Commerce	www.doc.gov
Department of Defense	www.defenselink.mil
Department of Energy	www.energy.gov
Department of the Interior	www.doi.gov
Department of Transportation	www.dot.gov
Agency for Toxic Substances and Disease Registry	www.atsdr.cdc.gov
Bureau of Land Management	www.blm.gov
Bureau of Reclamation	www.usbr.gov
Army Corps of Engineers	www.usace.army.mil
Council on Environmental Quality	www.whitehouse.gov/CEQ
Environmental Protection Agency	www.epa.gov
Federal Energy Regulatory Commission	www.ferc.fed.us
Federal Highway Administration	www.fhwa.dot.gov
Fish and Wildlife Service	www.fws.gov
Food and Drug Administration	www.fda.gov
Government Printing Office	www.gpo.gov
National Oceanic and Atmospheric Administration	www.noaa.gov
National Park Service	www.nps.gov
National Science Foundation	www.nsf.gov

Occupational Health and
Safety Administration   www.osha.gov
Office of Surface Mining www.osmre.gov
General Accounting Office www.gao.gov

The Federal Web Locator at www.infoctr.edu/fwl can provide
Internet addresses and linkages to other agencies.

Some other sites of interest include the following:

- thomas.loc.gov—The Library of Congress maintains this
  legislative service named for Thomas Jefferson. It
  contains bills, legislative history, Congressional record
  references, links to bill sponsors, reports, and
  accompanying documents back to 1973.

- www.ntis.org—The National Technical Information
  Service can provide information about and copies of
  numerous environmental documents.

- www.findlaw.com—This legal reference site contains an
  index of and linkages to laws, codes, law reviews, legal
  organizations, and law school information.

- www4.law.cornell.edu/uscode—The Cornell Law School
  Legal Information Institute has a *U.S. Code* website with
  an update service providing recent changes to particular
  code sections.

There is an ongoing stream of new books about how to use
the Internet for legal research. See, for example, JOSHUA D.
BLACKMAN (WITH DAVID JANK), THE INTERNET FACT FINDER
FOR LAWYERS: HOW TO FIND ANYTHING ON THE NET (1998),
and DON MACLEOD, THE INTERNET GUIDE FOR LEGAL
RESEARCH (2d ed. 1997). Check these or newer books for
more information.

APPENDIX B:
MAJOR FEDERAL ENVIRONMENTAL LAWS AND REGULATIONS

The following is a list of major federal environmental laws. Listed under each law are key programs and regulations that may result in the generation of environmental documents.

As discussed in the "Statutes" section of Chapter 2 ("Preparing to Comment"), federal environmental laws are printed in the *United States Code* (U.S.C.). The following table lists the citation to the full text of the law across from the name of the statute. The first number is the "title" number; it appears on the spine of each volume. The second is the number of the section or sections ("§" is the section symbol—two of them mean two or more sections).

There is one problem. People in environmental law invariably refer to statutes by yet another number: the section number in the bill as passed by Congress before placement in the U.S.C. For example, the EIS provisions of NEPA began life as statutory section 102 before incorporation into U.S.C. as 42 U.S.C. §4332. Most people still call it 102 (i.e., one, oh, two). In the table below, these numbers appear in parentheses following the names of the key programs or provisions. The U.S.C. provision is listed beside it. You may need either or both to find what you need or understand what you read.

The following table also contains citations to the pertinent regulations in the *Code of Federal Regulations* (C.F.R.). As above, the first number refers to the "title" number that appears on the spine of each volume. The C.F.R. is divided into "Parts" with sections within each part. Again, the section symbol (§)

designates sections. If you see, for example, a citation to 40 C.F.R. §6.604, look up Title 40, Part 6, Section 6.604.

CLEAN AIR ACT
42 U.S.C. §§7401-7671q

State Implementation Plans (§110)   42 U.S.C. §7410
                                         40 C.F.R. Part 51

New Source Permits (§§172, 173)   42 U.S.C. §§7502, 7503
                                         40 C.F.R. Parts 70, 71

CLEAN WATER ACT
33 U.S.C. §§1251-1387

State Water Quality Management   33 U.S.C. §§1288, 1313(e)
Plans (§§208, 303(e))   40 C.F.R. Part 130

National Pollutant Discharge   33 U.S.C. §1342
Elimination System Permits (§402)   40 C.F.R. Parts 122, 123, 125, 129

Dredge or Fill Permits (§404)   33 U.S.C. §1344
                                         40 C.F.R. Parts 230-233
                                         33 C.F.R. Parts 320-330

COASTAL ZONE MANAGEMENT ACT
16 U.S.C. §§1451-1465

Coastal Zone Management   16 U.S.C. §1455
Programs (§306)   15 C.F.R. Part 923

Coastal Nonpoint Pollution   16 U.S.C. §1455b
Control Programs (§306A)

COMPREHENSIVE ENVIRONMENTAL RESPONSE, COMPENSATION, AND LIABILITY ACT
42 U.S.C. §§9601-9675

Emergency Response (§106)   42 U.S.C. §9606
                                         40 C.F.R. Part 300

Remedial Investigation/Feasibility   42 U.S.C. §§9606, 9621
Studies and Proposed Plans   40 C.F.R. Part 300
(§§106, 121)

Settlements (§122)   42 U.S.C. §9622

EMERGENCY PLANNING AND COMMUNITY RIGHT-TO-KNOW ACT
42 U.S.C. §§11001-11050

Emergency Plans and   42 U.S.C. §§11003, 11004
Notification (§§303, 304)   40 C.F.R. Part 355

Reporting Requirements   42 U.S.C. §§11021, 11022, 11023
(§§311, 312, 313)   40 C.F.R. Parts 370, 372, 373

ENDANGERED SPECIES ACT
16 U.S.C. §§1531-1544

Endangered and Threatened   16 U.S.C. §1533
Species Determinations (§4)   50 C.F.R. Part 17

FEDERAL INSECTICIDE, FUNGICIDE, AND RODENTICIDE ACT
7 U.S.C. §§136-136y

Pesticide Registrations (§3)   7 U.S.C. §136a
                               40 C.F.R. Parts 152-155, 158

Reregistrations (§4)   7 U.S.C. §136a-1
                               40 C.F.R. Part 152

Administrative Reviews   7 U.S.C. §136d
and Suspensions (§6)   40 C.F.R. Part 164

FEDERAL LAND POLICY AND MANAGEMENT ACT
43 U.S.C. §§1701-1785

Land Use Plans (§202)   43 U.S.C. §1712
                               43 C.F.R. Part 1600

Sales of Public Lands (§203)   43 U.S.C. §1713
                               43 C.F.R. Part 2710

Withdrawals of Lands (§204)   43 U.S.C. §1714
                               43 C.F.R. Part 2300

Exchanges of Lands (§206)   43 U.S.C. §1716
                                   43 C.F.R. Part 2200

Grazing Leases and Permits (§402) 43 U.S.C. §1752
                                   43 C.F.R. Part 4100

MARINE PROTECTION, RESEARCH, AND SANCTUARIES ACT
33 U.S.C. §§1401-1434

Ocean Dumping Permits   33 U.S.C. §§1412, 1414
(§§102, 104)   33 C.F.R. Part 324
                                   40 C.F.R. Parts 220-225, 227, 228

NATIONAL ENVIRONMENTAL POLICY ACT
42 U.S.C. §§4321-4370d

Environmental Impact   42 U.S.C. §4332
Statements (§102)   40 C.F.R. Parts 1500-1508
                                   Each agency has its own regulations[40]

NATIONAL FOREST MANAGEMENT ACT
16 U.S.C. §§1600-1687

National Forest System Land and   16 U.S.C. §1604
Resource Management Plans (§6)   36 C.F.R. Part 219

RESOURCE CONSERVATION AND RECOVERY ACT
42 U.S.C. §§6901-6992k

Hazardous Waste,   42 U.S.C. §6925
Treatment, Storage, or   40 C.F.R. Part 270
Disposal Permits (§3005)

Solid Waste Plans (§4003)   42 U.S.C. §6943
                                   40 C.F.R. Parts 256-258

---

40. For a comprehensive list of citations to agency NEPA regulations, see NICHOLAS C. YOST, NEPA DESKBOOK, 2d Edition 104-06 (1995).

SURFACE MINING CONTROL AND RECLAMATION ACT
30 U.S.C. §§1201-1328

Surface Coal Mining Permits (§506)	30 U.S.C. §1256
	30 C.F.R. Parts 773, 774

TOXIC SUBSTANCES CONTROL ACT
15 U.S.C. §§2601-2692

Manufacturing and	15 U.S.C. §2604
Processing Notices (§5)	40 C.F.R. Parts 720, 721

Appendix C:
Making a Freedom of
Information Act Request

Under the Freedom of Information Act (FOIA), federal agencies must make records available to you, unless the records are specifically exempt from disclosure.[41] Each agency has its own FOIA regulations.[42] Under these regulations, the term "records" is generally very broad and the exemptions are relatively narrow.[43] You will probably be able to see more paper than you can stand, if you follow the right procedures.

The first step is making a FOIA request. This should be done in writing or through a FOIA link on an agency website.

Articulating what records you want is the hardest part. How do you get the good stuff and not the junk? A narrow request is good because you may get access to material more quickly. You don't want to overwhelm the agency (it may be your buddy or your buddy's contractor who has to respond). Also, the time to respond to a big request may be longer, and, as discussed below,

---

41. Freedom of Information Act, 5 U.S.C. §552(a), (b), *available in* ELR Stat. Admin. Proc.

42. *See, e.g.,* Freedom of Information Act Procedures, 40 C.F.R. pt. 1515 (1999) (Council on Environmental Quality); Records and Testimony, Freedom of Information Act, 43 C.F.R. pt. 2 (1999) (Department of the Interior); Public Information, 40 C.F.R. pt. 2 (1999) (EPA).

43. *Compare, e.g.,* 40 C.F.R. §2.100(b) (EPA definition of "record") *with* 40 C.F.R. §§2.118, .119 (definition of exemption categories and discretionary release). Agencies may try to withhold so-called "enforcement sensitive" and "pre-decisional" documents.

you may have to pay for search time and copying. On the other hand, a broad request is good because you might find some really neat things that you did not know to ask for. You're on your own for this.

The letter should go to the agency's FOI Officer. You can find the address of the FOI officer on the agency's website, in the agency FOI regulations, or by telephoning the agency and asking. There is a central FOI Officer at the agency's main office, and there may be officers in regional or local offices as well. For example, each EPA region has its own FOI Officer handling regional matters. If you want essentially local rather than national information, and there is a local FOI Officer, write or e-mail the local Officer. To be nice, and perhaps speed things up a bit, send a courtesy copy of your request to your buddy or at least to someone at the office where you think the documents are (ask if you don't know).

The FOI Officer will log in your request, and the government then has 20 working days to respond.[44] EPA and Department of Interior regulations allow 10 working days for an "initial determination," and the government may give itself a 10-working-day extension, if it needs one.[45] (It may take longer for a big request.) When the government responds, it may send you a copy of the documents or make them available for your review at its offices. It will also identify any documents covered by your request that it believes are exempt from disclosure.[46] If you have asked for voluminous material, the agency may contact

---

44. 5 U.S.C. §552(a)(6)(A)(i), *available in* ELR STAT. ADMIN. PROC. Note that FOIA requires agencies to promulgate regulations providing for expedited processing of requests, if the requestor demonstrates a compelling need. *Id.* §555(a)(6)(E).

45. 40 C.F.R. §2.112(a), (e); 43 C.F.R. 2.17(a), (c).

46. You can appeal this determination, if you disagree. *See, e.g.,* 40 C.F.R. §2.114.

you to discuss the fees and see if you will narrow your request or indicate a maximum fee. One option may be for you to review files at the agency and tag for copying the documents you want.

Exercise caution with your requests as the government can charge both for search time and copying. Agency regulations specify the FOIA charges, which vary from agency to agency and sometimes for different categories of requesters. Agencies may also have provisions for waiver of fees in certain instances or a policy concerning availability of information. For example, EPA NEPA regulations state that "[t]o the maximum extent practicable, materials made available to the public shall be provided without charge. . . . "[47] Read the pertinent provisions closely, check with your buddy and/or the FOI Officer, and follow the procedures to make sure that you aren't surprised by a whopping FOIA bill.

---

47. Procedures for Implementing the Requirements of the Council on Environmental Quality on the National Environmental Policy Act, 40 C.F.R. §6.402(a) (1999).